Rethinking Criminology: The Realist Debate

Sage Contemporary Criminology

Series editors

John Lea ● Roger Matthews ● Jock Young

Sage Contemporary Criminology draws on the best of current work in criminology and socio-legal studies, both in Britain and internationally, to provide lecturers, students and policy-makers with the latest research on the functioning of the criminal justice and legal systems. Individual titles will cover a wide span of issues such as new developments in informal justice; changing forms of policing and crime prevention; the impact of crime in the inner city; and the role of the legal system in relation to social divisions by gender and race. Throughout, the series will relate theoretical problems in the social analysis of deviancy and social control to the practical and policy-related issues in criminology and law.

Already published

Jeanne Gregory, *Sex, Race and the Law: Legislating for Equality*
John Pitts, *The Politics of Juvenile Crime*
Roger Matthews (ed.), *Informal Justice?*
Nigel South, *Policing for Profit: The Private Security Sector*
Roger Matthews (ed.), *Privatizing Criminal Justice*
Tony Vass, *Alternatives to Prison*

Rethinking Criminology: The Realist Debate is a companion volume to *Issues in Realist Criminology* edited by Roger Matthews and Jock Young

Rethinking Criminology:
The Realist Debate

edited by
Jock Young and Roger Matthews

SAGE Publications
London • Newbury Park • New Delhi

SAGE Publications Ltd
6 Bonhill Street
London EC2A 4PU

SAGE Publications Inc
2455 Teller Road
Newbury Park, California 91320

SAGE Publications India Pvt Ltd
32, M-Block Market
Greater Kailash – I
New Delhi 110 048

British Library Cataloguing in Publication data
Rethinking Criminology: Realist Debate. —
(Sage Contemporary Criminology Series)
I. Young, Jock II. Matthews, Roger III. Series 364

ISBN 0-8039-8620-3
ISBN 0-8039-8621-1 (Pbk)

Two-volume set: *Rethinking Criminology*
ISBN 0-8039-8484-7
ISBN 0-8039-8485-7 (Pbk)

Library of Congress catalog card number 92-050109

Typeset by GCS, Leighton Buzzard, Bedfordshire
Printed in Great Britain by Hartnolls Ltd, Bodmin, Cornwall

Contents

Contributors

John Lea, Centre for Criminology, Middlesex Polytechnic.

John Lowman, School of Criminology, Simon Fraser University.

Roger Matthews, Centre for the Study of Public Order, Leicester University.

Vincenzo Ruggiero, School of Social Work, Middlesex Polytechnic; Department of Sociology, University of Bologna.

Ian Taylor, Department of Sociology, University of Salford.

Jock Young, Centre for Criminology, Middlesex Polytechnic.

1 Reflections on realism

Roger Matthews and Jock Young

The emergent writings of radical realist criminology have been widely associated with the rise of Thatcherism in Britain. Thatcherism no doubt created a number of new problems and challenges, but criminological realism was not simply a product of governmentality; rather they were both a product of changing socioeconomic conditions during the 1970s. In the field of 'law and order', the problem of crime and its control had begun to take on new dimensions and significance. When asked on the eve of the 1979 election whether she would make 'law and order' a central issue, Margaret Thatcher replied, with some justification, that it was not she but the British public which would ensure that this issue was given priority. Numerous opinion polls carried out over the next decade indicated that the problem of crime was consistently found to be second only to unemployment as a cause of public concern.

On one side there had been a persistent rise in the number of recorded offences; increasing almost fivefold between 1960 and 1980, despite the overall increase in welfare expenditure (Bottoms, 1987; Hough and Mayhew, 1985; Radzinowitz and King, 1977). On the other side, most of the principal agencies involved in the criminal justice process appeared increasingly unaccountable, inefficient and costly. There was a growing problem of delivering the required services to an increasing number of victims of crime.

The police, in particular, who were popularly seen as being in the front line of the 'fight against crime' were identified as the primary agency for reorganization. Consequently, much of the effort expended during the early 1980s by policy makers and criminologists was aimed at improving police performance and increasing accountability (Reiner, 1985; Kinsey et al., 1986). Subsequently other agencies – prison officers, probation officers, and to a lesser extent the judiciary – have come under review. Unfortunately, during the 1980s crime continued to rise – increasing from 2.6 million recorded offences in 1980 to over 4 million in 1990 – while the leading agencies, despite attempts to change their organization and practices, continue to present serious problems in terms of performance and accountability.

Victimization studies have shown that the impact of crime is uneven. It falls disproportionately on the poorer and more vulnerable sections of the population and serves to compound the growing economic and social inequalities which have risen dramatically over the past decade. Paradoxically, it is the more disadvantaged groups who pay a disproportionate amount of the cost of financing an increasingly costly criminal justice system. As Ian Taylor argued so forcibly at the beginning of the 1980s the differential impact of victimization, the compounding of other inequalities, and the disorganizing effects of crime on communities mean that 'law and order' should more properly be viewed as a left rather than a right-wing issue, and that there is a pressing need to reformulate left social democratic response which is in touch with the real fears and anxieties of its constituent groups (Taylor, 1981).

The growing problems associated with crime and its control have created new situations and challenges for criminologists. The priority accorded to the issue has meant that it has become more difficult to remain purely contemplative and politically disengaged. A promising development in Britain has been the formulation of a range of competing policies from those to the left of the conventional conservative–liberal framework. Some of these, admittedly, have suffered from being over-defensive and reactive, but there have been encouraging signs among left social democratic groupings that the issue of crime control is being conceived within an alternative political framework which stresses different priorities, values and objectives (Birley and Bright, 1985).

Developing consistent and viable alternative methods of crime control can be a daunting task. But these problems have been compounded in Britain over the past decade by the swings and variations in government policies. The Thatcherite policy has been diverse, uneven, and at times clearly contradictory. The 'get tough' policies, for example, which were widely publicized at the beginning of the decade, have been substantially reviewed. Although punitiveness has remained an essential ingredient of conservative policy, it has increasingly been conditioned by fiscal concerns as well as the development of more 'privatized' and corporatist responses in some areas (Matthews, 1989; Pratt, 1989).

The net effect of these different and competing strands has been the production of a peculiar mix of policies. There has been the toughening up of responses to certain categories of offenders and a softening of others. By the same token increased prison sentences for some have been accompanied by the increased use of cautioning and diversion for others. Often implicit in these bifurcated strategies are contradictory assumptions concerning the aetiology of crime and the dynamics of intervention (Bottoms, 1977). A massive prison-building programme has occurred in a period that has witnessed a levelling off in the custodial population. Funding for the police has increased 60 percent over a decade in which police performance has dropped consistently, and against a background of official publications which have stressed that extra police and resources are likely to provide minimum advantages in terms of crime control (Heal et al., 1985). Most remarkably, despite the massive increase in public and private expenditure on crime control during the 1980s, crime has continued to rise to unprecedented levels (HMSO, 1988).

These paradoxes of policy suggest that it would be incorrect to see recent government policy in Britain as involving simply the exercise of increased repression or as representing a form of 'authoritarian populism' (Hall et al., 1978; Jessop et al., 1987). Neither of these terms adequately captures the vicissitudes of recent right-wing policies, and consequently they offer little help in understanding, combating or providing alternatives to these policies.

Thatcherism itself is, however, only one particular manifestation of an international political shift which has placed various 'new right' administrations in power in a number of western countries during the 1980s. Some countries, such as Britain, have experienced a peculiar political transformation in which the power of the parties of the centre has declined as well as those on the Marxist left. This has created new political alignments and a sharpened opposition between right and left social democratic parties. These changing political configurations have been translated into criminological discourse, which has in the process become repoliticized. As liberal reformism and forms of non-interventionism on one hand and Marxist fundamentalism and reductionism on the other appear less credible new tendencies have emerged, issues have been reformulated and the parameters of the debate have shifted.

Alongside these political changes, which have set new agendas in criminology, there has been a general crisis in criminological theory. This crisis has at least four dimensions. The first is what has been referred to as an aetiological crisis (Young, 1986). The second dimension involves a crisis of identity, that is, a profound uncertainty about its own development and its future direction. The third level of crisis arises from its underlying androcentrism and the inapplicability of a wide range of existing criminological theory to women (Leonard, 1982). The final dimension relates to the low level of policy relevance of much criminological investigation. As John Braithwaite recently commented:

> The present state of criminology is one of abject failure in its own terms. We cannot say anything convincing to the community about the causes of crime; we cannot prescribe policies that will work to reduce crime; we

cannot in all honesty say that societies spending more on criminological research get better criminal justice policies than those that spend little or nothing on criminology. Certainly we can say some important things about justice, but philosophers and jurists were making a good fist of those points before ever a criminological research establishment was created. (Braithwaite, 1989: 133)

In place of a coherent causal and structural account of contemporary developments there has been a shift towards administrative and instrumental approaches. The policies which have emanated from these developments have apparently been to redistribute rather than reduce crime: These strategies, which have undoubtedly been fostered by the 'new right', have often been narrowly focused, poorly co-ordinated and badly monitored (Rosenbaum, 1988; Young, 1986).

The growing realization through the decade that these limited policies, with their weak theoretical base, were not providing an adequate response to the problems of crime and its control has encouraged the development of alternative approaches which offer a broader focus and firmer foundation. Radical realism in Britain is an attempt to respond to this challenge. It is 'radical' in a number of senses. First, the perceived seriousness of crime is such that it requires a response which goes beyond piecemeal engineering and short-term adjustments. Secondly, the term 'radical' is meant to convey the construction of a political response which is not subsumed within the traditional liberal–conservative consensus. Thirdly, it is radical in that it sees the need to tackle the problem of crime 'at root'. That is, it sees the need for a more comprehensive theoretical framework which can uncover the underlying processes that produce these problems and to provide a more solid basis for designing interventions. Lastly, it considers itself to be radical in the sense that it draws freely on a tradition of critical theorizing which aims to demystify and dereify social relations.

The term realism is meant to indicate the creation of criminology which while remaining 'radical' is simultaneously competing and applied. It is a criminology which expresses a commitment to detailed empirical investigation, recognizes the objectivity of crime, faces up to the damaging and disorganizing effects of crime, and emphasizes the possibility and desirability of engaging in progressive reform (Matthews, 1987a).

There is some encouraging evidence of alternative approaches to the problem of crime emerging in a number of different countries. There seems to be a growing recognition that there is an urgent need for the construction of a criminology which is both 'radical' and 'realistic', although the particular formulation and adoption of these themes will vary from country to country (see Chapters 5 and 6).

We have seen over the last two decades new influential neo-conservative criminologists who have fed directly into the policy programmes of 'new right' administrations. The so-called 'new realists' in America, for example, who have significantly influenced criminal justice policy in that country, represent a formidable intellectual tendency (Platt and Takagi, 1977). This group of 'realists', which includes some of the best-selling English-speaking criminological writers in the world such as James Q. Wilson (1983) and Ernest van den Haag (1975), has wittingly and unwittingly been confused with radical or left realists.

Left and right realism

Although there are some points of overlap between the 'new realists' and the 'radical realists', these two approaches represent distinctly different theoretical and political positions. They share a concern with the corrosive effects which crime can have on communities and with the formulation of workable policies, but they are ultimately oppositional and competing positions.

They differ in a number of important respects. First, the new realists tend to take conventional definitions of crime for granted. Radical realists on the other hand, although adopting the general categories of crime as their point of departure, are not constrained by either commonsensical definitions nor by official modes of prioritization. Rather, the issue of 'seriousness' and significance of different crimes is seen as the object of investigation. By the same token it employs a much wider frame of reference than 'new realism' which concentrates almost exclusively on 'street crime'. Radical realism has, through the use of victimization surveys, sought to broaden the parameters of enquiry and has more recently begun to examine a range of 'white-collar' and occupational offences (Pearce and Tombs, 1992).

Secondly, there are substantial differences in the type of explanations that are offered – particularly in relation to the question of causality. James Q. Wilson, for example, expresses reservations about what he sees as the search for 'deep' causes, offering instead in his book with Richard Herrnstein, *Crime and Human Nature* (1985), a behaviouristic theory of conditioning. Crime is, they maintain, ultimately a function of trans-historical 'human nature'. As a result their analysis lacks a social economic context and is excessively individualized. The relation between the individual and society and the role of socioeconomic processes in structuring choices and opportunities is conveniently played down (see Chapter 4).

The absence of a material context for social action and a lack of appreciation of the socioeconomic constituents of crime allows the 'new realists' to operate with a predominantly voluntaristic conception of the criminal and to embrace essentially punitive policies aimed at controlling the 'wicked'. Thus the import of the analysis offered by writers like Wilson and van den Haag is to encourage an overemphasis on control and containment to the exclusion of more thoughtful and constructive policies (Currie, 1985). As we have seen in recent years, however, there has been a formal movement away from the type of punitive policies advocated by the 'new realists' in a number of western countries, not because of any ideological difficulties, but because they have been found to be ineffective, inappropriate and too expensive – even by right-wing administrations.

Left realism then is the opposite of right realism. Whereas realists of the right prioritize order over justice, left realists prioritize social justice as a way of achieving a fair and orderly society. Whereas right realists descend to genetic and individualistic theories to blame the 'underclass', left realists point to the social injustice which marginalizes considerable sections of the population and engenders crime. If the two realisms have anything in common it is the rejection of utopianism: there are no magical solutions; all interventions in the control of crime have a social cost which must be weighed against their effectiveness.

Right realism is a new right philosophy: left realism stems from the current debates in democratic socialism. Thus it argues that only socialist intervention will fundamentally reduce the causes of crime, rooted as they are in social inequality, that only the universalistic provision of crime prevention will guard the poor against crime, that only a genuinely democratic control of the police force will ensure that community safety is achieved.

Thus on one hand, left realism takes an oppositional political and theoretical stance from that adopted by the realists of the right; while on the other it consciously avoids collapsing into the romanticism and idealism which has been evident in much of the radical and critical criminological literature of the 1970s.

Radical criminology and radical realism

It is easy to lose sight of the contribution which radical criminology played in shaping the nature of the debate in the 1960s and 1970s. Radical criminology provided many of the concepts and terms which were effective in opposing mechanistic conceptions of crime and deviance, while scrutinizing and exposing state (mal)practices. It offered a wider framework of analysis which was able to explore the social, political, ideological, economic and historical dimensions of crime and control. It challenged the dominant conceptions of crime and punishment, offered new perspectives, and attempted to develop a sustained critique of the operation of the criminal justice system.

Although radical criminology pointed to the weakness, omissions and errors of conventional criminology it was never able to offer a competing alternative. Its critique was essentially negative and reactive. Unable to offer a feasible alternative it was always destined to operate as the bad conscience of conventional criminology (Cohen, 1979).

As the influence of Marxism on social thought began to recede during the 1980s and the parties on the far left declined or disappeared, a serious revision of left-wing social and political thought was unavoidable. In the realm of theory the two major changes which occurred which most directly affected the radical criminological project involved the discrediting of orthodox Marxist theories of the state and its conception of power. The influential writings of Michel Foucault challenged the view, held by many on the left, that power was essentially negative and repressive, and that it operated primarily on a coercion–consent continuum (Foucault, 1979; Poulantzas, 1978). The related view that the state was merely 'the executive committee of the bourgeoisie', acting as an instrument of class domination and thus destined to disappear after the revolution, was also viewed with growing scepticism.

Within the ranks of radical criminology divisions began to appear and various factions emerged. Radical criminologists soon became acutely aware that a generation of students that they had taught to be critical had ended up by criticizing them. Students and practitioners increasingly wanted answers to problems which existing forms of radical criminology seemed unable to supply. The value of radical criminology became measured less in terms of the number of new concepts it could generate and more in terms of the range of social problems which it tried to solve. Theoretically and politically, the forms shifted towards developing more pluralistic and democratic forms of control. 'Social control' ceased to be a negative concept and an undesirable process. Instead, the problem increasingly became one of trying to make control more social.

As the right attempted to dismantle parts of the state apparatus, the need to defend the positive and protective elements of state intervention became glaringly obvious to the majority of socialists. A range of state provision was seen as not only necessary but desirable in order to compensate for the vagaries of the market and to mediate growing inequalities. The debate on the left turned increasingly towards improving the quality and level of services while minimizing the repressive aspects of the state. The political challenge was to develop those state forms which would increase people's collective level of security but which did not unduly restrict their freedom.

Within radical criminology a number of divisions appeared in relation to the analysis of state agencies – particularly in the criminal justice arena. Some radicals remained ideologically committed to the abolition of the criminal justice system. Defending aspects of state provision, or arguing for the expansion of services, was seen by the abolitionists as an error which served inadvertently to relegitimate the criminal justice system. Some radical criminologists seemed to be arguing that the criminal justice system should be dismantled because it did not work, while on other occasions they claimed that it worked only too well. Some found a useful compromise in the form of negative functionalism which claimed that institutions such as the prison tend to 'succeed' throughout their perpetual 'failure' (Foucault, 1977; Reiman, 1979).

A parallel set of propositions which is frequently mobilized by radicals claims that on one hand progressive reform is virtually impossible, while maintaining on the other that where reforms are seen to be effective they only serve to relegitimize the system. This type of double-bind has been most evident in the recent debate on informal justice (Matthews, 1988).

Thus, central to the debates between radical criminologists is the notion of reform and in particular the meaning of progressive reform. For the realists the recognition that crime is largely intra- rather than inter-class, with the poor paying dearly for inadequate protection, the need to improve the effectiveness of criminal justice agencies seems obvious. For the abolitionists who believe that the notion of 'crime' is something of a fiction and that the criminal justice system is only capable of repression there is no justification for maintaining formal criminal justice agencies. Indeed they are even critical of the realists' emphasis on the need to create a more accountable and efficient system of policing and imprisonment (Mathiesen, 1990; Hulsman, 1986; Brown and Hogg, 1992).

Where realists and abolitionists do appear to share some common ground is in their belief that radical criminology should aim for the integration of theory and practice. How such integration should be achieved was one of the central themes in radical thinking throughout the 1960s and 1970s. The majority of radical criminologists during this period were never seriously interested in engaging in a detailed investigation of crime or in developing policies to control it. Instead they concentrated on the process of 'criminalization' and of providing a range of theoretical critiques of official policy (Young, 1988). Thus, in the area of criminology the relation between theory and practice was left largely unexplored and the balance tilted heavily in the direction of theory.

In a recent paper which attempts to examine the significance of left realism within the radical criminological tradition, Stanley Cohen has proposed an alternative vision of the relation between theory and practice which is designed both to foster theoretical investigation while pursuing concrete interventions. In this way he aims to reconcile some of the differences between realism and idealism (Cohen, 1990).

Cohen raises the problem of whether the preoccupation with the integration of theory and practice has been misplaced. There are, he argues, different levels of investigation and intervention which are not always directly compatible. Theoretical investigation may not always be 'relevant' but this does not make it any less legitimate a pursuit. We have to balance, he argues, the scepticism and uncertainties of theoretical enquiry with the need to engage in practical interventions to reduce crime, inequalities and injustices. 'Surely', he argues, 'it is possible to be sceptical and ironical at the level of theory – yet at the level of policy and politics to be firmly committed'. Thus Cohen tries to square the circle of engaging in intellectual doubt while dealing with immediate practical issues.

There are two main problems which arise in relation to this approach. First, the depiction of intellectual and academic life as being bound up with a 'spirit of scepticism, doubt and uncertainty' in which answers are invariably provisional and uncertain, while political life is seen as being more precise and calculable, is in an important respect a misleading caricature. In a sense, it is in the realm of theory that the prospect of improving consistency and coherence in an otherwise uncertain and ever-changing world appears possible. The identification of irony and ambiguity is not the abnegation of this search but part of its articulation. Even ardent advocates of irrationalism and scepticism employ rational and logical arguments to demonstrate the coherence of their position. The practical world on the other hand is beset by contingencies, complexities and uncertainties. Intervention is always an extremely precarious business. For every sceptical academic there is an equally sceptical bureaucrat. When reform 'fails' it is just as likely to be due to the problems of intervention as to the limitations of the theory.

The second point which arises from this discussion concerns the possibility and desirability of integrating theory and practice. We may well agree that theorizing and intervention can occur at any number of levels and that reconciling these differences may not always be possible. However, the issue is to what extent we should continue to strive for consistency between theory and practice or whether we should simply learn to live with the contradictions. This question is further complicated by the 'fact' that a range of 'practical' and 'political' interventions take place at the 'theoretical' level. The struggle around ideas and ideologies, the process of classification, the setting of policy agendas, and the articulation of objectives are no less 'practical' than implementing crime reduction strategies or reorganizing policing operations.

But it is precisely because the more abstract levels of theory set the frame of reference in which the sites and strategies of intervention are selected, and in which certain issues and objectives are prioritized, that the aim of trying to integrate theory and practice remains a necessary exercise. Even the most immediate and specific problem will raise a complex array of theoretical issues. Thus, it is not the case, as Cohen seems to imply, that 'confronting crime' involves a relatively low of theorizing. Developing a response to domestic violence or rape necessarily involves intensive debates about gender relations, patriarchy, state power, as well as on a range of legal and jurisprudential problems. It may well be the case that much recent criminological theorizing has been conducted at a conspicuously low level, but the attempt by some administrative and managerial forms of criminology to 'bracket off' some of the wider theoretical issues is far from a necessary element in criminology. One of the aims of radical realism is to contribute towards the elaboration of these theoretical issues while developing an integrated approach which aims to combine practical achievements with a socialist politics.

This is not to privilege theory over practice or vice versa. It is to suggest, however, that ideas do not arise out of thin air, and that practical engagement, on whatever level, is a crucial component in forming, testing and shaping ideas. Much of the best work which has come out of the radical criminological tradition has arisen from practical involvement and from attempts to devise workable and progressive policies (Box, 1987; Carlen, 1990; Pearson, 1987; Pitts, 1990).

The relation between theory and practice is also obscured to some extent by Cohen's preoccupation with the notion of deconstruction. For Cohen it would seem that we are all deconstructionists now. But this term which has become closely associated with the emergence of postmodernism does not fit easily into the vocabulary of realism, which involves a qualified reaffirmation of modernism.

Realism and modernism

To some extent the elevation of the notion of 'deconstruction', by which is meant taking apart and questioning apparent unities over the notion of 'immanent critique' which has been elaborated for some time by critical theorists, and which is primarily concerned with understanding the dynamics of social processes, signifies an important shift within the social sciences. Critical theorists have tended to assume that one needs to understand the inner workings of phenomena in order to improve them. Deconstructionism, on the other hand, seems to offer no such promise. The relation beween theory and practice becomes more tenuous and the focus shifts to the 'reading' of texts and calls into question the 'illusions' of fixed systems of representation. Not surprisingly, writers like Foucault who have been extremely influential in the development of postmodernism have focused on the exploration of the ways in which knowledge is produced and constituted through a multiplicity of power relations in diverse settings. Thus Foucault's work with homosexuals and prisoners was not aimed at producing substantial reforms in state practices despite the 'totalizing' nature of his critique, but was instead dedicated to the cultivation of localized resistance to the institutions, techniques, and discourses of 'social control' (Foucault, 1977; Merquior, 1985).

Strangely enough, however, despite the undeniable influence of Foucault in the fields of criminology and penology, postmodern ideas have until recently had only a minimal impact on these subjects. This might be viewed as a positive feature if it were not that the slowness with which postmodernism has permeated criminology may largely be due to the current low level of theoretical debate in the subject. Paradoxically, it is just as postmodernism appears to be falling out of favour in the spheres of architecture and literature that it is beginning to make an impact on criminology (Harvey, 1989).

Advocates of postmodernism have launched a critique of criminology in general and left realism in particular. They have begun to question the meaning of 'progress' within criminology and are particularly sceptical of 'totalizing' and 'essentialist' theorizing.

The charge of essentialism has been levelled on a number of occasions (Brown and Hogg, 1992; Carlen, 1992). It is charged with treating the concept of crime as an essential unity and with trying to formulate a general theory of crime from the study of a range of problems which have nothing more in common than that they happen to involve violations of the criminal law. Carol Smart, for example, argues that criminology cannot deconstruct crime without deconstructing itself: she states that:

> The thing that criminology cannot do is deconstruct crime. It cannot locate rape or child sexual abuse in the domain of sexuality, nor theft in the domain of economic activity, nor drug use in the domain of health, to do so would be to abandon criminology to sociology, but more important it would involve abandoning the idea of a unified problem which requires a unified solution – at least at the theoretical level. (Smart, 1990: 77)

The immediate problem with this type of critique is that of infinite regress. We might ask Smart in turn what she means by (essentialist) categories such as 'rape' and child abuse (which themselves could be endlessly deconstructed) or why rape might be better (causally?) explained in terms of sexuality rather than as a crime. But as left realists have argued, the categories of crime are neither arbitrary nor accidental. They arise from definite social and historical relations and it is erroneous to 'assume that the state can create definitions and categories "at will" quite independently of those established by popular social communication' (Lea, 1987, 1990). This does not mean that one should treat such categories uncritically but to emphasize that they have a social base and cannot be defined away.

This critique of essentialism therefore seems to raise considerable problems of its own. We also feel that when applied specifically to left realism it is largely misplaced. One of the unifying themes within the left realist project has been the problematization of crime, and to overcome the one-sidedness of those criminologies which have only addressed one aspect of what has been referred to as 'the square of crime' – the offender, the victim, the state and the public.

We shall return to this issue below since we feel that an elaboration of these complex processes of action and reaction through which 'crime' is constructed is a fundamental element in any viable criminology. Pursuing this objective, however, leads us directly into a further confrontation with those postmodernists who express disdain for what they call 'grand narratives'. Such totalizing accounts, they argue, lose sight of the multiplicity and diversity of modern power relations and can lead to totalizing regimes.

As we have already suggested, contemporary criminology is characterized by this lack of 'grand narratives' and has become increasingly fragmented and instrumentalist over the last decade or so. This, as left realists have argued, has impaired the coherence and value of criminological investigation (Young, 1986). At the same time, however, we have argued for specificity and warned against the dangers of 'globalism' (Matthews, 1987b; and see Chapter 2). These aims are not incompatible. On the contrary, an adequate explanation of crime and control needs to incorporate the particular and the general, and to locate specific and discrete phenomena within a framework which locates and explains the relation between the parts. It is a serious error of the relativists and nominalists who argue that the divergent and contingent nature of crime makes a general theory of crime impossible. The aim of a general theory of crime is to explain the diversity and the apparently contingent nature of criminal events and to show how these apparently arbitrary events are linked within identifiable processes.

Postmodernism often presents itself as a thoroughgoing critique, challenging the values and categories of conventional, modernist literature. It is far from clear, on examination, to what extent it actually represents a break with modernism (Callinicos, 1990). Its scepticism about 'progress', its deconstructing of the concept of crime, its antipathy towards grand theory, mean that it can too easily lead towards nihilism, cynicism and conservatism. Carol Smart, for example, claims that her critique of modernism and left realism 'does not entail a denial of poverty, inequality, repression, racism, sexual violence and so on', but she provides little indication of how any of these problems might be practically addressed. Challenging existing values and categories has a long and distinguished history, but if these values are simply rejected and not replaced with alternative visions then we become stranded and helpless. Postmodernism at this point turns into a pseudo-radicalism and becomes thoroughly depoliticized. It becomes ultimately a conservative stance, which is unable to offer any directives for social change and in which the concept of emancipation has no place.

Rather than modernity having failed, the truth is that it has never been fully implemented. It is an as yet unfinished project which has encouraged considerable gains in the fields of political justice, science, art and aesthetic experience. To abandon these gains would undoubtedly be regressive. Postmodernism thus appears at best as a compensatory strategy representing the 'dark side' of the modernist project (Habermas, 1990).

Our defence of modernism, however, is not uncritical. We would concur with the critiques of technicism and of instrumentalism which have accompanied developments in art and science, just as we, in conjunction with other modernists, scrutinize such notions as progress. Taking such a critical stance, however, does not mean that we do not think that there has not been, or cannot be, progress (Alexander and Sztompka, 1990).

The postmodernist critique of criminology melts into air. It offers deconstruction rather than reconstruction. By dismissing the 'essentialist' concept of 'crime' (everything has to be placed in parentheses) the principal object of criminology is removed and the subject is dissolved into larger 'essentialist' disciplines such as sociology. Even the subcategories of crime disappear (rape, murder, theft, etc) for the same reasons. Ultimately writers like Smart, having dispensed with 'criminology' and its modernist variants in the form of 'left realism', and proceed to deny the logic of a 'feminist criminology'. Not surprisingly, a number of feminists have distanced themselves from this position (Lovibond, 1989). Strangely enough, however, the postmodernist critique has indicated some points of overlap between left realist and feminist criminology.

Realism and feminist criminology

Although there is some uncertainty about exactly what is meant by 'feminist criminology', there can be little doubt that the impact of feminists on criminological thinking has been one of the most productive and progressive inputs into the subject over the last decade or so (Leonard, 1982; Gregory, 1986; Eaton, 1986; Stanko, 1985; Carlen, 1988; Daly and Chesney-Lind, 1988). Feminists have challenged conventional criminology on every level – theory, strategy, method and politics. Through a variety of struggles a number of important gains have been made, particularly in relation to violence against women, both in 'public' and 'private' spheres (O'Donovan, 1985).

The existing array of literature written by or for women defies easy classification. But it is possible to locate this growing body of literature along two broad trajectories – the political and the epistemological/ theoretical. On the political front a range of broad classifications are normally used for the range of options – conservative, liberal, radical and socialist feminists. (These positions can be used to designate the political positions with which particular writers identify as well as those with which they are attributed.) On the epistemological dimension feminist contributions have been divided into three general groups – postmodernist, standpoint feminist and empiricist (Harding, 1990). The links between these epistemological and political positions is uncertain and can take various forms, but an exploration of this relation indicates some dimensions of the relation between left realism and feminist criminology.

If we begin with a discussion of epistemology it is with the group which Sandra Harding refers to as 'empiricist' that left realism most closely identifies. Some of the differences between postmodernism and left realism, with its commitment to a qualified modernism, have already been identified. In opposition to postmodernism, realism expounds an objectivism. It maintains that the processes of reasoned and rational debate are a necessary feature of any democratic social system, expresses a commitment to progress and, in particular, argues that the delivery of services on which the poor and powerless depend can, and should, be improved. It is not that we reject postmodernism out of hand, but it is, as we have argued, a great deal less novel and innovative than its supporters claim. The problematization of science, objectivity, rationality and the like have been well-worked themes within the modernist tradition. Postmodernists use the same tools of reason, logic and language, as those used by the modernists whom they criticize. They operate, as it were, within the same 'discursive formation' and they do not represent a break with modernism, but provide at certain times a compensatory position and at other times an inverted form of modernism.

An alternative to postmodernism is offered by what has become known as 'standpoint feminism'. This position has certain advantages in that it distances itself from the relativism and subjectivism of postmodernism and offers instead a sense of objectivism. From this position knowledge is a function of the 'standpoint' or the location of the collective subject and argues that instead of understanding particular programmes in terms of their 'social value', they should be evaluated from the standpoint of the group or class with which the author identifies.

The most prominent advocate of this position within the field of criminology and law is Maureen Cain, who has presented a version of standpoint feminism in opposition to the anti-essentialism of postmodernism on one side and what is seen as the ultimate androcentrism of 'empiricist' feminism on the other. Standpoint feminism starts from the premise that different social groups speak from distinctly different social locations and experiences. Cain argues that 'knowing from a feminist standpoint is not the same and indeed precludes knowing from a working-class or a black standpoint' (Cain, 1990). This approach raises two immediate questions. The first is the objective problem of how to reconcile class, gender and racial determinants in terms of, say, criminal activity. The second is the subjective problem that a significant body of people transverse these various standpoints. Some people, for example, may want to speak as black working-class women. The overriding problem from this position is that people from the same standpoint do not only speak with the same voice but often speak with competing and oppositional voices. How do we know which voices are authentic? The problem is compounded when it is stated that some men can be feminists. It suggests that the relationship between knowledge and interests is not unmediated. The question then arises of explaining how people of different, and even oppositional, social locations and experiences can come to see the world in generally similar ways. The considerable degree of consensus which is repeatedly reported in relation to the question of the 'seriousness' of crime among all social groups would be difficult to explain from the 'standpoint' position.

Cain is very reticent however to acknowledge the contribution which men have made or could make to 'feminist criminology'. How do we assess the contribution of male writers on subjects like prostitution, pornography, interpersonal violence, abortion and the like? The dismissal of any substantive contribution of men to feminist criminology appears as an attempt to counter the perceived androcentric nature of criminology with its opposite. It replaces one form of particularity with another. Ultimately, Cain appears to be more interested in constructing a particular form of feminism rather than a criminology, and in the process produces, like Smart, an anti-criminology.

As Pat Carlen (1992) points out, these brands of anti-criminology are reminiscent of some of the Marxist-influenced radical criminologies which were around in the 1970s and which aimed to dissolve criminology into the class struggle. Some of these arguments are also reminiscent of those crude versions of Marxism which claimed that 'the truth' was an expression of the theory of the working class.

Left realists have argued against such concepts of the state and epistemology for some time. It is also in opposition to writers like Cain and Smart who want to dissolve criminology into some other discipline, whether it be sociology, philosophy or politics. Both these writers seem to overlook that all subject areas overlap with others. There are no clear-cut boundaries. At a certain point medicine turns into moral philosophy, economics into politics, and politics into philosophy. The issue is whether the study of crime and the analysis of the operation of the criminal justice system provides enough of a unifying focus of investigation to treat it as a relatively autonomous subject area. We think that it does, and that it provides a unique and important area of investigation. It is unfortunate that influential writers like Cain and Smart should be in the process of abandoning criminology at a point where real gains are beginning to be made and where issues relating to women are becoming more predominant.

Those mostly responsible for promoting these struggles and debates within criminology are the so-called 'empiricists'. This term is used in a somewhat misleading way by Harding in her attempt to group all those who engage in 'empirical' research together. The general accusation levelled against this group is that they continue to operate within an androcentric paradigm which takes men ('malestream') as the norm and relies on common ('co-man') sense.

The caricature of all feminists engaged in empirical investigations as making the same basic assumptions or in taking men as the essential point of reference is grossly deficient. Within this large and diverse group there is a range of methods and strategies, and much of this work is premised on the questioning of forms of male domination. There is nothing essentially androcentric about engaging in detailed empirical investigation. On the contrary much recent feminist work has sought to undermine forms of male domination and to take the needs and concerns of women as its point of departure.

The critical issues are determining the validity and appropriateness of different forms of empirical enquiry and the relation between the approaches which have been developed by left realism and their relevance for the development of a feminist criminology. Sandra Walklate (1992) distinguishes between conventional, realist and critical victimology which she claims embody different views of women and which imply different policies and political implications. Although she acknowledges that left realists may have contributed to uncovering important aspects of female victimization through local crime surveys, she argues that feminist criminology would be better served by a critical victimology which could 'uncover the layers of reality which structure both experience and a response to this particular form of victimisation'. In essence, she is arguing that, by concentrating on the most immediate impact of crime rather than exploring in depth the layers of women's experiences, realism ends up by not being 'realist' enough. Realists would reply to this charge that, although they may not wholly embrace the kind of essence/appearance division suggested by Walklate, they claim no monopoly of the 'real' and would have no opposition to approaches (feminist realist?) which offered the possibilities of a deeper understanding.

On the political dimension left realism has affinities with feminists who do not espouse a separatist politics but who see the women's struggle as part of a broader collective process of emancipation. It would be possible to present a more detailed matrix of the political and epistemological dimensions of feminist criminology and to locate the range of authors more precisely. The links between theory and politics is not always clear but it is possible to identify some affinity between standpoint feminism and radical feminism, for example, and between the postmodernists and those forms of political scepticism which, while having radical pretentions, turn ultimately into conservatism.

One issue which remains central to both realists and feminists is the definition of crime. The definitional issue has always been a stumbling block within criminology. Often criminologists have relied on simplistic definitions of crime and seen it as an 'act', or alternatively they have denied the significance of the act and claimed that it is a function of the 'reaction'. In attempting to move beyond these limited oppositions, realism has begun to examine the processes of action and reaction through what has become termed 'the square of crime'.

The square of crime

The notion of the square of crime is a shorthand which has emerged in the writings of criminological realism and is designed to serve as a reminder that 'crime' arises at the intersection of a number of lines of force. It is therefore an important antidote to those who see crime solely in terms of victims and offenders and ignore the role of the state and public opinion. At the same time it serves as a critique of those who see the process of 'criminalization' as a wholly state-generated process.

The growing interest in victimization and the recognition of the intimate relations which are often evident between victims and offenders has made this part of the equation a more accepted feature of the analysis. However, the role of the state and public opinion is less well understood. As we have seen with respect to radical criminology, when the state has been referred to it has been predominantly depicted as a repressive and essentially coercive instrument. But under the influence of writers like Foucault, the conception of the state and underlying notions of power have been challenged (Foucault, 1979). As a result there is now a greater sensitivity to the productive and constructive aspects of state control.

Within the square of crime the role and significance of public opinion has been generally neglected. Left realists, however, in arguing for a more democratic and responsive criminal justice system have begun to consider the role of public opinion and community controls in the construction and regulation of crime. The examination of police practices and crime figures indicates the critical role of public tolerance in defining and reporting incidents to the police (Kinsey et al., 1986). Similarly, work on penal reform has raised the question of the relation between public attitudes and sentencing policies as well as the important role public opinion plays in influencing the penal 'climate' (Graham, 1990; Downes, 1988).

Realism argues against both the tendency of experts to tell the public what are its real problems and the 'subjectivist' approach, which believes that crime priorities can be simply deduced by reading off the computer printouts of public opinion surveys (see Chapter 2). It maintains that, particularly in the inner city, direct public experience of many crimes generates both rational priorities as to the problem faced and realistic fears. It sets its face against the conventional wisdom that women and the elderly are prone to irrational fears and that the fear of crime is more of a problem than crime itself (see Sparks, 1992). This being said, the influence of a sensationalist mass media creates public anxiety in the areas of which the public have little direct experience. For example, in terms of crime, 'crack' has been projected as a considerable problem in Europe despite the fact that there is a low level of cocaine use. This is even more evident in the areas of crime control, where public conceptions of measures such as neighbourhood watch and 'stop and search' are beset by unrealistic assessments of their effectiveness.

The role of criminologists is to debate with the public over crime priorities: it is neither to reflect nor bestow public problems. The role of realism is to situate the problem of crime within its social context. John Lea (Chapter 3) demonstrates the argument that the nature of the relations within the square and the construction of different 'crimes' is a function of the balance of forces within the square. This perspective

avoids, we would argue, the charge of 'essentialism' and si\
taneously avoids the notion that crime is purely a product of definit\
as labelling theorists would argue. Rather, it is a complex proces_ _
action and reaction. Unpacking these dynamics allows us to move
beyond the one-sided characteristics of much contemporary criminology.

But as Vincenzo Ruggiero (Chapter 5) points out, the notion of the
square of crime omits the important dimension of criminological
theorizing itself. It therefore remains largely unreflexive and unable to
properly locate its own role in the process. On examining the square
of crime more closely we also become aware that the relation between
state and civil society and victim and offender are of a different order
and a different magnitude. Not only is the relationship between these
component parts asymmetrical, it is also that the significance of the
victim–offender relationship is 'over-determined' by the wider relations between the state and civil society.

Further, a missing dimension of the victim–offender relation is that
of space. The context in which victim–offender relations occur are
critical to the meaning of such interactions. It is not only as the
positivists claim that crimes are concentrated in certain locations, it is
also that in different locations acts may more readily be defined as
crimes. Thus the social context within which acts occur gives them
meaning, although this is not to deny that there may well be a
prevalence of certain acts in certain contexts (Smith, 1986).

Thus the square of crime on closer examination takes on a different
and more complex shape. If we were to try to express this relation
diagrammatically, it would take something like the form shown in
Figure 1.1. The notion of the square of crime thus remains an
important reminder of the various processes through which 'crime' is
constructed and a useful device for avoiding the one-sidedness of most
contemporary accounts.

Conclusion

The commentaries on left realism which have appeared to date have
been diverse and often contradictory. On one side left realism has been
seen as misdirected and focusing on the wrong issues; while on the
other side it is accused of presenting nothing new and as being merely
old wine in new bottles.

We have tried to indicate that left realism does offer a distinctly
different approach to the analysis of the processes through which
crime is constructed, one which avoids the excesses of idealism and
essentialism. Realism argues that previous criminological theories
have been partial. That is, they only focus on one part of the square of

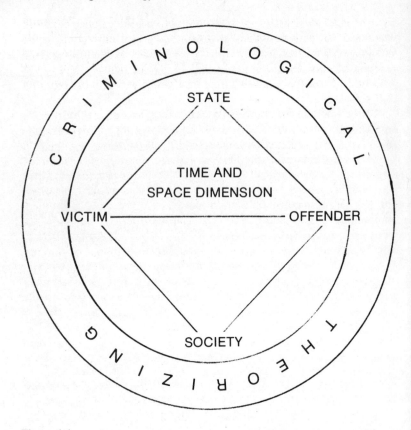

Figure 1.1

crime: the state (as in labelling theory, neo-classicism), the public (as in control theory), the offender (as in positivism) or the victim (as in victimology). One of its major aims is to provide an analysis of crime on all levels and to develop where possible a range of policy recommendations. It does not aim, however, simply to synthesize the existing disparate range of criminologies, but rather to develop a coherent analysis which touches upon these diverse positions.

Realism is critical of the extremely simplistic notions of causality implicit in traditional social democratic theory, the inadequate theorization of the central categories of the state and 'public opinion', and the lamentable standards of evaluation used in monitoring interventions. It refuses to be drawn into the defeatism and pessimism associated with some current strands of 'radical' theorizing, particularly in the form of postmodernism, and expresses a qualified commitment to the modernist project, by attempting to develop a coherent and reasoned analysis which incorporates 'grand narratives' while recognizing the need for specificity. It retains a commitment to problem solving, to the improvement of service delivery and to the provision of a more equitable, responsive and accountable criminal justice system.

Finally, left realism involves the repoliticization of crime. It maintains that crime cannot be effectively reduced through individualistic, technicist or administrative policies as the neo-conservatives suggest. Rather, crime reduction requires, as radical criminology has always argued, an appreciation of a wide range of political and structural processes which go beyond the boundaries of conventional criminology. This does not mean that nothing can be done short of a fundamental transformation of the social structure, but that the effectiveness of particular strategies is likely to be conditioned by these wider processes. Criminology is drawn ineluctably, therefore, into the wider political realm, and crime control must inevitably become part of a comprehensive political programme. For too long we have pretended it could be otherwise.

References

Alexander, T. and Sztompka, P. (eds) (1990) *Rethinking Progress*. London: Unwin Hyman.

Birley, D. and Bright, J. (1985) *Crime in the Community: Towards a Labour Party Policy on Crime Prevention and Public Safety*. Labour Campaign for Criminal Justice.

Bottoms, A. (1977) 'Reflections on the renaissance of dangerousness', *Howard Journal*, 16(2): 70–96.

Bottoms, A. (1987) 'Reflections on the criminological enterprise', *Cambridge Law Journal*, 42(2): 240–63.

Box, S. (1987) *Recession, Crime and Punishment*. London: Macmillan.

Braithwaite, J. (1989) 'The state of criminology: theoretical decay or renaissance?', *Australian and New Zealand Journal of Criminology*, September: 129–35.

Brown, D. and Hogg, R. (1992) 'Law and order politics', in R. Matthews and J. Young (eds), *Issues in Realist Criminology*. London: Sage.

Cain, M. (1990) 'Towards transgression: new directions in feminist criminology', *International Journal of the Sociology of Law*, 18(1): 1–18.

Callinicos, A. (1990) *Against Postmodernism*. London: Polity Press.

Carlen, P. (1988) *Women, Crime and Poverty*. Milton Keynes: Open University Press.

Carlen, P. (1990) *Alternatives to Women's Imprisonment*. Milton Keynes: Open University Press.

Carlen, P. (1992) 'Criminal women and criminal justice: the limits to, and potential of, feminist and left realist perspectives', in R. Matthews and J. Young (eds), *Issues in Realist Criminology*. London: Sage.

Cohen, S. (1979) 'Guilt, justice and tolerance: some old concepts for a new criminology', in D. Downs and P. Rock (eds), *Deviant Interpretations*. Oxford: Martin Robertson.

Cohen, S. (1990) 'Intellectual scepticism and political commitment: the case of radical criminology'. Paper presented at William Bonger Memorial, University of Amsterdam.

Currie, E. (1985) *Confronting Crime*. New York: Pantheon Books.

Daly, K. and Chesney-Lind, M. (1988) 'Feminism and criminology', *Justice Quarterly*, 5(4): 497–538.

Downes, D. (1988) *Contrasts in Tolerance*. Oxford: Clarendon.

Eaton, M. (1986) *Justice for Women? Family Court and Social Control*. Milton Keynes: Open University Press.

Foucault, M. (1977) *Discipline and Punish: The Birth of the Prison*. London: Allen Lane.

Foucault, M. (1979) *The History of Sexuality: An Introduction*. London: Allen Lane.

Graham, J. (1990) 'Decarceration in the Federal Republic of Germany', *British Journal of Criminology*, 30(2): 150–71.

Gregory, J. (1986) 'Sex, class and crime: towards a non-sexist criminology', in R. Matthews and J. Young (eds), *Confronting Crime*. London: Sage.

HMSO (1988) *The Costs of Crime*. London: HMSO.

Habermas, J. (1990) *The Philosophical Discourses of Modernity*. London: Polity Press.

Hall, S., Chritcher, S., Jefferson, T., Clarke, J. and Roberts, B. (1978) *Policing the Crisis*. London: Macmillan.

Harding, S. (1990) 'Feminism, science and anti-enlightenment critiques', in L. Nicholson (ed.), *Feminism/Postmodernism*. London: Routledge.

Harvey, D. (1989) *The Condition of Postmodernism*. Oxford: Blackwell.

Heal, K., Tarling, R. and Burrows, J. (eds) (1985) *Policing Today*. London: HMSO.

Herrnstein, R. and Wilson, J. (1985) *Crime and Human Nature*. New York: Basic Books.

Hough, M. and Mayhew, P. (1985) *Taking Account of Crime*. London: HMSO.

Hulsman, L. (1986) 'Critical criminology and the concept of crime', *Contemporary Crises*, 10: 63–90.

Jessop, B., Bonnett, K., Bromley, S. and Ling, T. (1987) 'Popular capitalism: flexible accumulation and left strategy', *New Left Review*, 165: 104–22.

Kinsey, R., Lea, J. and Young, J. (1986) *Losing the Fight Against Crime*. Oxford: Blackwell.

Lea, J. (1987) 'Left realism: a defence', *Contemporary Crises*, 11: 357–70.

Lea, J. (1990) *In Defence of Criminology: A Reply to Carol Smart*. Middlesex Polytechnic: Centre for Criminology.

Leonard, E. (1982) *Women, Crime and Society*. London: Longman.

Lovibond, S. (1989) 'Feminism and postmodernism', *New Left Review*, 178: 6–28.

Mathiesen, T. (1990) *Prison on Trial*. London: Sage.

Matthews, R. (1987a) 'Taking realist criminology seriously', *Contemporary Crises*, 11: 371–401.

Matthews, R. (1987b) 'Decarceration and social control: fantasies and realities', in J. Lowman et al. (eds), *Transcarceration*. Aldershot: Gower.

Matthews, R. (1988) *Informal Justice?* London: Sage.

Matthews, R. (1989) 'Privatization in perspective', in R. Matthews (ed.), *Privatizing Criminal Justice*. London: Sage.

Merquior, J. (1985) *Foucault*. London: Fontana, Modern Masters.

O'Donovan, G.C. (1985) *Sexual Divisions and the Law*. London: Wiedenfeld and Nicolson.

Pearce, F. and Tombs, S. (1992) 'Realism and corporate crime', in R. Matthews and J. Young (eds), *Issues in Realist Criminology*. London: Sage.

Pearson, G. (1987) *The New Heroin Users*. Oxford: Blackwell.

Pitts, J. (1990) *Working with Young Offenders*. London: Macmillan.

Platt, A. and Takagi, P. (1977) 'Intellectuals for law and order: a critique of new realists', *Crime and Social Justice*, Fall-Winter: 1–16.

Poulantzas, N. (1978) *State, Power and Socialism*. London: Verso.

Pratt, J. (1989) 'Corporatism: the third model of juvenile justice', *British Journal of Criminology*, 29(3): 219–42.

Radzinowitz, L. and King, J. (1977) *The Growth of Crime*. London: Hamish Hamilton.

Reiman, R. (1979) *The Rich Get Richer and the Poor Get Prison*. London: Wiley.

Reiner, R. (1985) *The Politics of the Police*. Brighton: Wheatsheaf.

Rosenbaum, D. (1988) 'Community crime prevention: a review of the literature', *Justice Quarterly*, 5(3): 323–95.

Smart, C. (1990) 'Feminist approaches to criminology, or postmodern woman meets atavistic man', in L. Gelsthorpe and A. Morris (eds), *Feminist Perspectives in Criminology*. Oxford: Oxford University Press.

Smith, S. (1986) *Crime, Space and Society*. Cambridge: CUP.

Sparks, R. (1992) 'Reason and unreason in "left realism": some problems in the constitution of the fear of crime', in R. Matthews and J. Young (eds), *Issues in Realist Criminology*. London: Sage.

Stanko, E. (1985) *Intimate Intrusions. Women's Experience of Male Violence*. London: Virago.

Taylor, I. (1981) *Law and Order: Arguments for Socialism*. London: Macmillan.

van den Haag, E. (1975) *Punishing Criminals*. New York: Basic Books.

Walklate, S. (1992) 'Appreciating the victim: conventional, realist or critical victim-ology?', in R. Matthews and J. Young (eds), *Issues in Realist Criminology*. London: Sage.

Wilson, J.Q. (1983) *Thinking about Crime* (2nd edn). New York: Vintage Books.

Young, J. (1986) 'The failure of criminology: the need for radical realism', in R. Matthews and J. Young (eds), *Confronting Crime*. London: Sage.

Young, J. (1988) 'Recent developments in criminology', in R. Haralambos (ed.), *Developments in Sociology* Vol. 4. Ormskirk: Causeway Press.

2 Ten points of realism

Jock Young

We have to deal, indeed, with an extensive and deeply-rooted social disease, which dug itself into the very body of society like a kind of ulcer; at times even threatening its very existence, but always harmful in the highest degree. Countless crimes are committed, and millions of criminals condemned, every year. Economically, the disadvantages to society are very great ... I think it is undeniable that crime is a source of stupendous waste of money to society. Next to the economic, we have, moreover, the still more important moral disadvantages. If criminality is closely bound up with the moral standards of a people, in return it sends out demoralizing influences towards the normal sections of the population. And when one adds to all this the damage and grief suffered by the victims of the crime, and also the constant menace which criminality constitutes to society, the total obtained is already a formidable one. Neither ought we to forget the suffering on the part of the criminal himself, who – in whatever way one may wish to judge him, is after all, a part of humanity too.

The reasons for the study of criminology should therefore be clear. Admittedly it is a science which is widely studied for its own sake, just like other sciences; crime and criminals are not a bit less interesting than stars or microbes. The element of *la science pour la science* should be present in every scientist, otherwise he will be no good in his profession; and this applies to the criminologist too. But this point of view is secondary as compared with the practical aspect, just as in the case of medical science. Indeed, comparison with the latter repeatedly suggests itself. Criminology ought before anything to show humanity the way to combat, and especially, prevent, crime. What is required more than anything is sound knowledge, whereas up to the present we have had far too much of dogma and dilettantism. (Bonger, 1935: 5–7)

The roots of realism
The last 20 years have witnessed a remarkable intensification of debate in criminology. The core problem has been the consistent rise in crime occurring in many, although by no means all, advanced industrial countries despite rapidly increasing standards of living coupled with the blatant ineffectiveness of the prisons and the growing awareness that extra police would only have a limited effect on the crime rate. I have detailed this process elsewhere (Young, 1986, 1988a). Suffice it to say that the two staple paradigms of criminology, social positivism

(better conditions reduce the crime rate) and neo-classicism (more, effective punishment diminishes crime), became increasingly untenable. There was a crisis in causality (the 'aetiological crisis') and in penality. It was in response to this that the various new criminologies developed: control theory, right realism, the new administrative criminology and left idealism. Central to all these theories was a radical reappraisal of the notion of social causality. For some the search for causes of crime were rejected outright, whereas for others causality was directed away from the political and economic structure of society to the moral climate of society or the family or on to the 'crime-prone' individual. And, whereas those on the right acknowledged, indeed exaggerated, the rise in crime while managing to disconnect this from a critique of the inequitable societies which generate crime, a wide spectrum of criminologists from the liberal centre to the left downplayed or actually denied the problem of crime.

Concomitant with this was a rise in public concern about crime. In particular a rise in sensitivity to violence occurred, with clear indications, in the case of Britain at least, that intolerance of violence increased faster than the actual rise in violent behaviour (Young, 1991). Feminists pointed to the problems of domestic violence against women, of rape, of harassment in work and public places and, more recently, the problem of child abuse. The Green movement made us conscious of pollution, of environmental blight, of the perils of nuclear contamination and of dumping: all of which have clear links with corporate crime and governmental deviance. Animal Rights activists pinpointed the violence inherent in factory farming and laboratory testing. Anti-racist and gay groups highlighted the increasing incidence of racial attacks, of 'gay-bashing' and of widespread harassment. The rise in public demand for a more humane society and for a more tolerable physical environment is a key social change of the last two decades. And if the rise in crime posed aetiological problems for criminology, so did the question of changes in what is tolerable behaviour and what could be done to achieve a more civilized society.

Public bureaucracies became the subject of increased scrutiny, both by the New Right and by Social Democrats intent on public accountability. The inefficiencies of public service provision became embodied in the notion of the public as a consumer, no longer willing to have problems bestowed upon them in the old Fabian tradition, but demanding value for money and effectiveness. The long rise of the consumer society engendered a public which demanded, not only in the private sector but in the public, qualitatively higher standards of service delivery (Corrigan et al., 1988).

Thus we can trace four major processes which have transformed criminological thinking: (1) the aetiological crisis as a consequence of rising crime rates; (2) the crisis in penality in terms of the failure of prisons and a reappraisal of the role of the police; (3) the increased awareness of victimization and of crimes which had previously been 'invisible'; (4) a growing public demand and criticism of public service efficiency and accountability.

Realism explicitly attempts to tackle all of these areas and to enter into debate with the responses of new right establishment criminology and left idealism. To a differing extent all of these problems and debates have been manifest in the recent history of advanced industrial societies. Of course, there are wide variations: in a few countries there has been little increase in crime, prison unrest and palpable ineffectiveness has not been universal, the new social movements which have entered into victim advocacy have developed unevenly, feminism has stronger traditions in certain countries than in others, the size of welfare bureaucracies varies, the configuration of social democratic and new right politics exist in different combinations, and so on. And, within the academy, criminology as a discipline exists with differing traditions and strengths. Thus, although the general problems which realism seeks to answer exist internationally in advanced industrial societies, their specific configuration depends on the political and social context of each country (see Brown and Hogg, 1991). In the introduction to this book we have traced the particular problematic in Britain. But although realist ideas have had a particular resonance in British criminology, they are by no means rooted in this context (cf. Taylor, Chapter 4). Nowhere is this more obvious than in Elliott Currie's seminal work, *Confronting Crime* (1985). This starts with the premise of the exceptional nature of American society as a prime cause of the extraordinarily high crime rate. This is no doubt correct, but the policy recommendations and domain assumptions which Currie makes are undoubtedly realist (see the interesting commentary by Marty Schwartz, 1990). Similarly, the recent 1990 Conference on Realist Criminology in Vancouver, hosted by Brian MacLean and John Lowman, involved debates between Australian, US and British scholars, raising mainly issues of convergence and disagreement, many of which related to different social and political contexts (see *Critical Criminologist*, 1990). But the general problematic was realist, and realism itself puts great stress, as I shall argue, on the relationship between general principles and specific conditions.

The principle of naturalism

The most fundamental tenet of realism is that criminology should be faithful to the nature of crime. That is, it should acknowledge the *form* of crime, the *social context* of crime, the *shape* of crime, its trajectory through *time*, and its enactment in *space*.

The form consists of two dyads, a *victim* and an *offender*, and of ~~actions~~ and ~~reactions: of crime~~ and ~~its control.~~ This deconstruction gives us four definitional elements of crime: a victim, an offender, formal control and informal control. Realism, then, points to a square of crime involving the interaction between police and other agencies of social control, the public, the offender and the victim (see Figure 2.1).

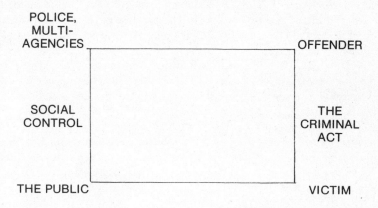

Figure 2.1

Crime rates are generated not merely by the interplay of these four factors, but as *social relationships* between each point on the square. It is the relationship between the police and the public which determines the efficacy of policing, the relationship between the victim and the offender which determines the impact of the crime, the relationship between the state and the offender which is a major factor in recidivism, etc. I shall return to this later, but suffice it to say that the relationship between the four points of the square (offender, victim, state agencies and the public) varies with differing types of crime (see Lea, Chapter 3). Indeed, a hallmark of critical criminology is its pinpointing of the irony of the frequent symbiotic relationships between control agencies – whether formal or informal – and crime. For example, the way in which the burgled public create the informal economy which sustains burglary, or the police create, through illegalities, a moral climate which spurs delinquents into crime.

Secondly, it should be stressed that, in pinpointing to the fact that crime rates are produced by such an interaction, one is merely describing the process. It does not involve acceptance of the existing patterns of criminalization.

Crime rates are a product, therefore, of changes in the number of putative offenders, the number of potential victims, and the changing levels of control exercised by the official agencies of control and the public. No explanation which does not embrace all these four factors can possibly explain crime rates. Let us focus quite simply, for the moment, on the relationship between social control in all its manifestations, and the criminal act consisting of the dyad of victim and offender.

If we examine changes over time: realists would point to these *necessarily* being a product of changes in criminal behaviour *and* changes in the sensitivity to crime. The increase in the rate of violent crime *by definition* must involve changes in violence. None of this makes it any the less 'real': for this is exactly what crime rates *really* are. This being said, the exponential increases in crimes occurring in most western countries cannot merely be a product of increased sensitivity to crime. Any dark figure of the crime unknown to the police would have been taken up long ago by the rise in crimes known to the police, and other indices, such as homicide rates and serious property crimes, indicate rises even if we use earlier thresholds as our measure. Thus present rises in rates of violence in countries such as England may well be a product of an increased sensitivity to violence *and* a rise in violent behaviour.

Realist criminology indicates that crime rates are a product of two forces: changes in behaviour and changes in definitions of what is seriously criminal. These two social dimensions are not necessarily co-variant. It is quite possible, for example, for vandalism to increase but people to become less concerned and more tolerant about litter, graffiti, etc. It is possible for acts of violence in a behavioural sense to decrease, yet people become more sensitive to violence.

The social context consists of the immediate social interaction of these four elements and the setting of each of them within the *wider* social structure. Such an agenda was set out within *The New Criminology* (Taylor et al., 1973), namely, that the immediate social origins of a deviant act should be set within its wider social context and that such an analysis should encompass both actors and reactors. Realism takes this a stage further, insisting not only that actions of offenders and the agencies of the state must be understood in such a fashion, but that this must be extended to the informal system of social control (the public) and to victims (see Young, 1987).

To turn to the shape of crime: crime is a series of relationships. Each type of crime presents a different network of relationships; if we compare illegal drug use, burglary and assault we note markedly different structures (see Figure 2.2).

Drug dealing has a well-known pyramidal shape; burglary involves numerous victims and regular fences; assault may well be a one-off case of victimization. Furthermore, the natural history of crime

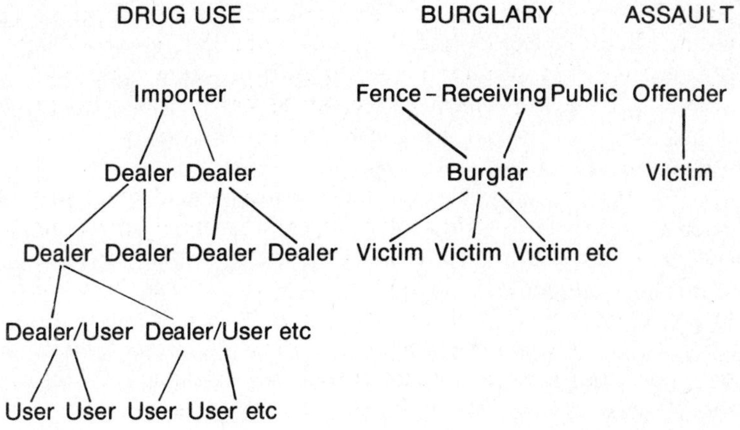

DRUG USE   BURGLARY   ASSAULT

Figure 2.2

involves differences in the content of these relationships. Crime involves both cooperation and coercion. In the case of drug use, every step of the pyramid is consensual; in the case of burglary, dealing in stolen goods is consensual and the actual act of stealing coercive; in the case of assault, it is a purely coercive act.

The temporal aspect of crime is the past of each of the four elements of the square of crime and their impact on each other in the future. A realist approach sees the development of criminal behaviour over time. It breaks down this trajectory of offending into its component parts and notes how different agencies interact. Thus we can talk of (1) the *background causes* of crime; (2) the *moral context* of opting for criminal behaviour; (3) the *situation of committing crime*; (4) the *detection of crime*; (5) the *response to the offender*; (6) the *response to the victim*. Criminal careers are built up by an interaction of the structural position the offender finds him or herself in and the administrative responses to his or her various offences. These involve both material changes in the offender's structural position and the exchange of ideas (or 'rationalizations') for offending (Cohen, 1965; Matza, 1964). But, of course, such moral careers are not confined to the offender. Other points of the square of crime change over time. Policing practices change in their interaction with offenders, the public's fear of crime in the city creates patterns of avoidance behaviour which consciously and unconsciously develop over time, victims – particularly repeated victims such as in cases of domestic violence – change the pattern of their life as a consequence of such an interaction.

The spatial dimension of crime is the material space in which this process enacts itself. All crime has a spatial dimension, and the geography of crime varies widely in terms of the specific crime. Drug dealing has an international dimension, a national distribution and a focus on specific areas of the city. Burglary occurs widely across a locality and subsists on a hidden economy which is locally based. Assault has no wider spatial dimension. It occurs, however, frequently in specific areas. For example, in terms of assault by a stranger, it has a pronounced geographical focus which is made evident, both in the incidence of assault and the fear of victimization, manifest in the avoidance of certain areas. Just, then, as specific crimes involve differing structures of relationships, they also involve particular structures in space.

Crime occurs privately and publicly and specific crimes are private at certain points of their structure and public at others. In the case of drug dealing, all aspects of the crime, apart from street level, are extremely private transactions. At the level of the opportunistic user, it is quasi-public; people must know who the dealers are, and they must, like any other 'shopkeepers', be relatively open to the public. In the case of burglary, the act itself is, apart from the brief circumspect act of breaking in, a private act: it occurs usually when the owner is out of his or her house, and when neighbours can see no suspicious activities. Subsequently the sale of stolen goods is quasi-public: it occurs publicly in shops which fence wittingly or unwittingly stolen goods or, in terms of direct public purchase, it occurs in the public areas of the pub or workplace. Assault in a public place is, by its very nature, an open event. Unlike domestic violence, it is coercion in the street, in a public house, or in some other public venue.

The principle of multiple aetiology

If we examine the square of crime, it is obvious that crime rates involve a fourfold aetiology. It involves the causes of offending (the traditional focus of criminology), the factors which make victims vulnerable (e.g. lifestyle analysis, Felson and Cohen, 1981), the social conditions which affect public levels of control and tolerance, and the social forces which propel the formal agencies such as the police. It is impossible to explain crime rates in terms of one of these causal sequences, although it is commonplace in criminological theory that such *partial* explanations are attempted. And, of course, such explanations must involve an *aetiological symmetry*: it is inadmissible, for example, to grant the police a different aetiological status than that of the delinquent. Such an explanatory scheme must detail the *immediate signs* of behaviour and set this within the *wider social origins* (Taylor et al., 1973).

The present period in criminology is characterized by a retreat from a discussion of wider social causes of offending. With a few notable exceptions (Currie, 1985; Braithwaite, 1979), the social democratic tradition of making the link between social structure and offending is severed. In part, this is a response of establishment criminology to new right goverments, which, quite clearly, wish to embrace theories which disconnect their policies from uses in the crime rates. The abandonment of interest in crime causation has been complex and manifold. Precisely because it covered a wide spectrum of politics and theory it was extremely effective. The British school of administrative criminology was doubtful about the validity of causes of 'dispositions' altogether. The realists of the right, such as James Q. Wilson, did not deny that there were causes of crime. Indeed, they outlined a plethora of causes (Wilson and Herrnstein, 1985). Rather, they point to the few 'causes' which can be altered without making social changes which would be politically unacceptable, which stresses the individual rather than the social causes of crime. Travis Hirschi (1969), in his influential 'control theory', abandons causation to the extent that it is identified with motivation. Cause metamorphoses from active desire into absence of restraint.

The question of aetiology was, therefore, not abandoned. What were played down were the causes of offending: the traditional focus of criminology. Other aetiologies took its place: the causes of lack of informal controls (control theory), the causes of changes in exposure to victimization (Felson and Cohen's emphasis on lifestyle), the causes of ineffective formal sanctions (Wilson's emphasis on the inadequacy of punishment). That is, the partial causality rooted in the offender characteristic of positivism, in all its varieties, became replaced by other partial causalities focused on other dimensions of the square of crime: informal social control, the victim or the formal system.

Top-down and bottom-up explanations
Such a partiality is apparent, not only in criminology of the right, but in criminology of the left. This is seen clearly in the tendency to explain changes in crime and differences in the crime rate between groups, either in terms of *top-down explanations* (changes in the administration of justice), or *bottom-up explanations* (in terms of changes in criminal behaviour). Yet if we are to have a fully developed criminology, we must logically have both a sociology of action and reaction. How can we explain, for example, the rise in the official rate of crimes of violence in the majority of advanced industrial countries in this century if we do not explain both changes in violent behaviour and changes in sensitivity to violence? A one-sided approach – so common – which focuses on one or the other is patently inadequate.

Deviance and control cannot be studied independently of each other. You cannot study changes in policing without changes in patterns of crime, the social control of women without changes in the behaviour of women, the impact of drug legislation without changes in drug use. Systems of social control profoundly affect deviance and changes in deviance patterns of control. The two items are necessary parts of the equation and both variables interact with each other.

Interpreting the criminal statistics

Such a principle must be applied also to the vexed question of the interpretation of the criminal statistics. For the left idealists the criminal statistics are an epiphenomena – they measure the activities of statistics-generating bodies (the police, the courts, etc.). They do not measure differences in criminal behaviour. Thus the differences in official crime rates between, say, working-class and middle-class delinquency, or black and white crime, or even, the differential between boys and girls, is seen as a clear indication of the prejudices of the social control agencies and little else. The best statistics, according to these authors, would be the prison statistics, for at least they give a reasonably accurate measure of who is in prison. Claims of a 'crime wave' and of significant changes in the quantity of crime over time are seen to be the product of recurrent moral panics, materially under-scored by the increase in the size of police forces which inevitably generate a greater volume of statistics (e.g. Gilroy and Sim, 1985).

In contrast, for conventional criminology, crime statistics are un-scientifically gathered and metaphysical in their categorization – but on the whole, and at least in their profiles of criminality which they yield, they reflect the true differences in crime between different groups and of changes in the extent of criminality over time.

For the realist the fundamental axiom is, as we have seen, that the reality of crime is a product of action and reaction. Someone acts in a given way and certain legal agencies of control react against them. This double process is central to the nature of crime and to attempt to separate one from the other and to believe that there is a true crime rate independent of the activities of reactors, is a clear fallacy. Thus the debate about whether crime statistics are either largely a function of the reaction of social control agencies or a function of the activities of offenders is chimerical. An 'either-or' approach to criminal statistics simply violates the reality of crime. Both processes must be involved and the weighting varies widely between different types of crime. It should be noted, however, that in the vast majority of serious crimes reported to the police by the public, therefore, realistically the overall criminal rate tends to be propelled more by the motor of public demand rather than by proactive policing: that is by public definition of deviancy rather than those held by the police.

Although realism would see crime rates as a product of the administration of criminal justice (the reaction to crime) and the social situation which produces criminal behaviour (the criminal act), it stresses the predominance of structure over administration. (Such an analysis would be true also of a realist approach to health or education.) To take the racial 'disproportionality' of prisons, for example, the greatest factor in the higher proportion of blacks is due to poverty, age structure and residence in the inner city rather than the bias of the system (Currie, 1985; Reiman, 1979).

Three caveats to this must be made: (a) the administrative bias against imprisoning corporate and white-collar criminals compared to those committing conventional crimes; (b) the pronounced bias in the minority of cases where proactive policy is involved (e.g. drug offences: see Blumstein, 1982); and (c) the extraordinary effect of imprisonment on long-term recidivism where, indeed, criminal justice administration becomes the major driving factor in their structural position.

Relative deprivation and crime
At this point let us turn to the substantive explanation of crime. Realism sees a major cause of criminal behaviour as relative deprivation. Crime can, therefore, occur anywhere in the social structure and at any period, affluent or otherwise – it is simply not dependent on absolute levels of deprivation or the level in the social structure of the offender (see Lea, Chapter 3). This being said, it is clear that parts of the poor, particularly the lower working class and certain ethnic minorities who are marginalized from the 'glittering prizes' of the wider society, experience a push towards crime that is greater than elsewhere in the structure (Lea and Young, 1984).

To put an emphasis on relative deprivation as a cause of crime is not to retreat into monocausality. Of course, there are many causes of crime. Even within the tradition of anomie theory, subcultural theorists have tended to give undue emphasis to relative deprivation, the disjunction of aspirations and opportunities, over anomie as a lack of limits, a product of an individualism, where "From top to bottom of the ladder, greed is aroused without knowing where to find its ultimate foothold. Nothing can colour it since its goal is far beyond all it can attain" (Durkheim, 1952: 256). And certainly one can contrast the anomie of the disadvantaged, which is largely concerned with relative deprivation, from the anomie of the advantaged, which is often a product of a limitless pursuit of money, status and power (Young, 1974; Simon and Gagnon, 1986; Taylor, 1990). This being said, relative deprivation is an extremely potent cause of crime, for it is:

1 not limited to lower working-class crime because relative deprivation can, and does, occur throughout the social structure (see Lea, this volume);

2 not merely concerned with economic crime because subcultures of
   violence among the poor and the violence of better-off men occur
   precisely as a response to relative economic deprivation;
3 not concerned with absolute poverty, and thus pinpoints the
   paradox of those crimes of the poor which focus on status goods.
   As Elizabeth Burney pointed out in her study of street robbery:
   'Poverty is, nevertheless, not the immediate motive for street crime,
   since most offenders do not lack necessities: rather, they crave
   luxuries. The outstanding characteristic of young street offenders is
   their avid adherence to a group "style", which dictates a very
   expensive level of brand-name dressing, financed by crime' (1990):
   63; see also Currie, 1990).

The implications of this understanding of causality are of vital importance. Specifically, we have in our cities conditions of unemployment with no foreseeable future for young people, and where the
concept of 'youth' merely extends itself into those aged 30 and beyond.
In such a situation relative deprivation is manifest, in the contrast with
the increasingly wealthy strata of those in work, and is underscored by
the gentrification of our large cities which allows comparison to be
easily available and, indeed, unavoidable.

The principle of specificity

Both positivism and the new administrative criminology seek generalizations which are independent of culture. A discussion of whether
maternal deprivation leads to crime, or if beat policing is effective,
would be typical endeavours. Left idealism, with its sense of the
obviousness of criminological generalization, enters the field of general
laws with an abandon which would alarm the most staunch positivist.
Of course unemployment leads to crime; it is self-evident that the
recession has led to the rise in heroin use among young people, and so
on. Such a mechanistic relationship between objective conditions and
human behaviour is absurd. It is central to a realist position that
objective conditions are interpreted through the specific subcultures of
groups involved. This is the nature of human experience and social
action. Generalization is possible, but only given specific cultural
conditions and social understandings. Thus, absolute deprivation
(poverty, unemployment, etc) is no guide to the genesis of crime. This
is the central failure of positivism, both in its aetiology and its policy
making. Relative deprivation, experienced injustice in certain limited
political situations, is at the root cause of crime.

   The utter vacuity of the general 'law': unemployment leads to crime,
is displayed when one considers the majority of the human race:
women, who have a very high rate of unemployment (in terms of non-

domestic labour) and extremely low crime rates. But unemployment *does* give rise to crime in certain circumstances. The failure of such positivism is seen in the Home Office study of the relationship between race and crime (Stevens and Willis, 1979). Here they found a positive correlation between white unemployment and the white rate of crime. But for blacks, the relationship was puzzling: for there was a negative correlation between black unemployment and certain sorts of black crime and 'somewhat surprisingly' the *white* unemployment rate was found to correlate highly with the *black* crime rate. 'A plausible interpretation', they note, 'seems hard to find' (p. 23). For, from the point of view of positivism, it is as if one pushed one table and the table next to it moved! But as John Lea and I have argued elsewhere, such a finding is by no means strange:

> As we have argued, there are no *direct* relationships between objective factors and behaviour. The experience of blacks in areas of high white unemployment may well be that of racial discrimination and scapegoating. Such an alienated sub-culture would have a considerable reason to break its lawful bonds with the wider society; it might also experience the demoralisation which is the basis of much criminality. In areas where there is massive black unemployment, there may be less basis for a comparison with whites and thus a relative lack of the frustration that leads to criminality. (1984: 160)

Such an analysis can be applied to generalization in a wide variety of areas. For example, in the field of drugs research I have argued for a socio-pharmacological approach. This rejects both the notion that the effects of drugs situation and the moral careers of drug users can be read, so to speak, positivistically from the pages of a pharmocopoeia or relativistically, that drug use is a mere function of culture alone. Rather, specific drugs have effects in particular cultural set-ups: the psychotropic nature of the drug both structures and is structured by the culture (Young, 1971). And in the field of subculture theory, Ward and Kassebaum (1966), in their pioneering study of women's prisons, cut through the debate around whether inmate subculture is transmitted on from the outside pre-prison culture of the prisoners, or is a functional product of 'the pains of imprisonment' while within the prison. By adding the crucial variable of gender to the discussion they have shown how the way in which the pains of imprisonment are experienced is a function of the gender subculture of the inmates. The 'same' prison (objective conditions) produces widely different subcultural solutions (human behaviour) dependent upon the subjective assessment of the inmates.

If we are to be wary about sociological generalizations within one nation at one time, then we should be all the more wary about general laws which attempt to cross historical periods and hop from examples in one country to another. A classic illustration of lack of specificity is Scull's decarceration thesis (1977) which empirically assumed that all forms of deviancy involving incarceration would pass through the same sequence (as if the reactions of the powerful would not vary with the specific deviance) and, even more oddly, that the British figures, which did not fully substantiate his thesis, were simply 'lagging behind' those of the United States. Here we see not only a generalization from one country to another, but from one category to another.

Thus, to be more precise, the problem of specificity refers to generalizing about crime, law or victimization from one country or one social group and assuming that one's conclusions apply to all countries or social groups. It is being unable to see how general variables come together in a very specific form in any particular situation. This results in work which is not only inadequate as a generalization, but is lacking in its ability to cope with what is special about the precise constellation of factors which delineate any particular situation. Specificity is a heuristic failure, both on the level of the general and the particular.

The three major problems of specificity which have dominated criminological thinking have operated on the level of both social category and nationality. The first is obviously the fashion in which male, working-class crime has been used to depict all criminality. We have seen how the impact of, first of all, radical and then feminist criminology has sharply dislodged such thinking. The consequences for theory have been enormous. The new empirical dimensions have far from worked themselves out yet through the maze of conventional theory.

The second is the depiction of crime in advanced industrial countries to describe crime in general. Colin Sumner, in a brilliant essay on crime and under-development (1982), rightly castigates those authors such as Clinard and Abbott (1973) who see crime in poor countries as just a replay of what has occurred in the west, and their general economic development as just a delayed natural evolution. He points to the way in which all the traditional criminological equations become over-turned when one begins to look at police behaviour, crimes of the powerful, crimes of the poor and of political oppositionists within the context of global imperialism. Such work has only just begun, but it is of the utmost importance that radical criminology makes a committed attempt to tackle the problems. No one else will. Positivism never did and the new administrative criminology sees itself as producing control generalizations which will apply anywhere, from the estates of New England to the streets of Soweto.

The third problem of specificity is a relatively recent phenomenon occurring in the post-1945 period, and that is the Americanization of criminology. It is important to realize the significance of the domination of US criminology on the criminologies of the rest of the world. The central paradox is that the vast output of the United States – often involving the most innovative work in the field – emerges from a country which is extremely atypical in terms of the majority of advanced industrial countries. The homicide rate, for example, is 14 times higher in Los Angeles than in London, and if we are to look for countries which have similar rates of violence to the United States it would be to Latin America, rather than any other industrial country, east or west. There are a series of atypical characteristics of the United States which may well relate to its exceptional crime rate. For example, its lack of social-democratic politics, its extremely high commitment to the American Dream version of meritocracy, its high emphasis on formal legal equality as an ideal, its remarkable ethnic pluralism, the extent and range of organized crime, the extent of ghettoization, etc (Currie, 1985, 1990). All of these factors are likely to have a profound effect on the theory generated in such a society. The theory of differential association, Mertonian anomie theory, neo-Chicagoan labelling theory, social control theory, are all illuminated if we begin to think how they fit so well such an exceptional state. This is not an argument for theoretical isolationism. There is no doubt that the United States has, in this century, produced by far the most important developments in theoretical criminology. It is to argue, however, that these theories cannot merely be transplanted to, say, a European context; they have to be transposed *carefully*.

The contradiction, then, is that the most influential work in criminology stems from one of the most atypical advanced industrial states. The extent of this paradox can, perhaps, be illustrated if we imagine that Japan became in the 1990s the leading producer of criminological work. Japan is, of course, an extremely atypical capitalist society – and in the area of crime it is the absolute opposite of the United States. Even by European standards the changes in the crime rate are remarkable. For example, from 1948 to 1982 the crime rate in Japan declined by 36 percent compared to a rise of 348 percent in England and Wales over the same period. And this was despite dramatic changes taking place in Japanese society: massive industrialization, vast internal movements of population, urbanization and general social upheaval (Government of Japan, 1983).

It would not be difficult to imagine the types of criminological theory which would emerge from Japan if it indeed dominated the field of criminology. At the bottom line one can imagine quite 'reasonable' theories which linked a rise in the standard of living with a drop in crime. And one can visualize, perhaps, with a certain *schadenfreude*, criminologists in Berkeley or New York trying to fit the evidence of their own country in the new dominant paradigm.

To argue for specificity is not to argue against empirical generalization. It is to say that generalization is possible within particular social orders concerning particular groups. Nor is it to argue that cross-cultural theories of crime are impossible – it is to say firmly that these theories find their resolution in specific societies. For example, the notion of relative deprivation as a theory of discontent, which results in crime in certain social and political circumstances, is one of great heuristic value. But there is a big jump between how the form and content of relative deprivation is experienced among boys in the Lower East Side of Manhattan, to how it is structured in terms of girls in Florence, Japanese youth in Tokyo or corporate criminals in Switzerland.

The principle of focusing on lived realities

Realism focuses on lived realities. It is concerned with the material problem which particular groups of people experience in terms of the major social axes of age, class, gender and race, and spatially with their locality. It is these structural parameters which give rise to subcultures. Realism has a close affinity with subcultural theory (Willis, 1977; Cohen, 1965). Subcultures are problem-solving devices which constantly arise as people in specific groups attempt to solve the structural problems which face them. The problems are evaluated in terms of the existing subculture and the subculture changes over time in order to *attempt* a solution to those perceived problems (see Lea and Young, 1984: ch. 3; Young, 1974). Crime is one form of subculture adaptation which occurs where material circumstances block cultural aspirations and where non-criminal alternatives are absent or less attractive.

The experiences of the public with regard to crime and policing cannot be reduced to global figures of the average risk rates of particular crimes or the 'normal' citizen's experience of policing. All evidence indicates that the impact of crime and policing is geographically and socially focused: it varies enormously by area and by the social group concerned. The reason the realists tend to select inner-city areas is to enable us to detail such experiences at the sharp end of policing, while comparing this to data derived from wider-based surveys of total cities and the country as a whole. The reason for the use of extremely high sampling is to be able to break down the impact of crime and policing in terms of its social focus: that is, on social groups based on the combination of age, class, gender and race. Such a high social focus corresponds more closely to the lived realities of different groups and subcultures of the population. Thus, just as it is inaccurate to generalize about crime and policing from gross figures based on large geographical areas, it is incorrect, even within particular areas, to talk in terms of, for example, 'all' young people, 'all' women, 'all' blacks, 'all' working-class people, etc (Schwartz, 1988). Generalizations which remain on such global levels frequently obfuscate quite contradictory experiences, generating statistics which often conceal vital differences of impact. We have shown in the *Second Islington Crime Survey* (Crawford et al., 1990), for example, how the introduction of age into the analysis of fear of crime by gender changes the usual generality of men having low fear of crime and women high. In fact, older women have a fear of crime rather like men in the middle age group, and younger women have a fear rather like old men. And, in the case of foot-stops by the police, it becomes evident that differentials based on race are much more complicated than the abstraction that blacks are more likely to be stopped than whites. No older black women in our sample were stopped. Young, white, women were over three times more likely to be stopped than older black men. And even the differential between young black men and young white men becomes remarkably narrowed when class is introduced into the equation. Such an approach in realist method is termed an awareness of the specificity of generalization, the need to base analysis firmly grounded in specific areas and social groups. It is in marked contrast to the approaches which try to explain differences in experience in terms of only one of the major social axes: age, class, gender, or race. Such reductionism, as exemplified by radical feminism or fundamentalist class analysis, simply does not fit the reality of social experience. This approach enables us to be more discriminate about generalization with regard to changes in modes of policing and methods of crime control. For example, in the debate about shifts from consensual to more coercive forms of policing (Lea and Young, 1984), it allows us to ascertain whether contradictory forces at work involving consensual policing of certain areas and groups and more coercive methods with others. Similarly, the probable efficacy of crime control measures such as beat policing or neighbourhood watch must be grounded in specific communities and locations.

Putting behaviour into context

Realism involves the invocation of rationality rooted in material circumstances. That is, it places the behaviour of the offender, the police officer, the victim and the public at large, in the actual material circumstances that each individual experiences (Lea and Young, 1984). This is not to say that people do not make mistakes in understanding the world, whether it is the behaviour of the police officer in stop and search, or the fear of crime of the citizen. Indeed, this is *ipso facto* the very nature of rational behaviour. Rather, it sets itself against an idealism which analyses people's beliefs and behaviour, primarily as a product of free-floating ideas and prejudices, whether a product of outside influences such as the mass media, or socially detached group values, or personal psychological attributes.

Realist method relates attitudes and beliefs to actually lived experience of material circumstances. For example, it attempts to explain police behaviour, not in terms of the enactment of a group of people with, say, authoritarian personalities, or a macho culture, or rigid 'them' and 'us' attitudes engendered at training school. All of these things may or may not be true, but they are not the primary determinants of police behaviour. To take a police patrol as an example: it is the actual nature of the police task, the experiences confronted in attempting to achieve objectives in the face of the opportunities and difficulties encountered on the job which is central to understanding the behaviour of patrolling officers. In this instance of police practice it cannot be deduced from legal rules nor from a free-floating 'cop culture' nor the autonomous prejudices of individual police officers. Realism attempts to put police practice, the interpretation of rules, the generation of an occupational culture, and the attitudes of individual officers, in its context. For example, stop and search procedures are largely ineffective at dealing with the crimes to which the legislation was directed: burglary, hard drug use and carrying weapons. Direct information, either gleaned from the public, or by detective work, would be needed in order to have a high yield from such a procedure. In the absence of such information, patrolling officers equipped with stop and search powers, and wishing to have at least some yield from their work, will, of necessity, target those groups which have high offending rates, particularly young, working-class males – black and white. As most people stopped will be perfectly innocent, such a trawling of a particular social group will inevitably create a counter-productive hostility in the target groups and accusations of unfairness, selectivity and prejudice. But it is the inadequate tools for the job and an ill-thought-out piece of legislation which creates the working context for the police, not merely the enactment of personal and cultural prejudice.

Social constructionism, positivism and everyday life
Realism, then, does not deal in abstractions: the principle of specificity demands that explanation be grounded. It is not just that the concept of 'crime' embraces a motley of types of behaviour and varieties of legal regulation; each 'type' of crime and each form of regulation must be specified if we are to make any progress in understanding their interaction. Opiate addiction, for example, can mean many different things in particular subcultures. Burglary can involve the rational calculation of the professional or the opportunism of the young lad.

Domestic violence can involve a variety of sub-species, each with its own life cycle. And, turning to social control, beat policing can involve many greatly different activities from the aggressive to the consensual; neighbourhood watch can be a uniting or a divisive intervention. All of this suggests the necessity of typologies which cut across legal or formal definitions, but, going further, that these typologies must be grounded in the particular lived realities of the phenomenon under investigation. It does not exclude generalization, it merely argues that generalization must be socially based and explanations which are abstracted out of context have very little chance of aetiological success because they ignore the very social context which determines them.

The principle of social control

The control of crime must reflect the nature of crime. That is, it involves informal and formal interventions on both the level of the offender and the victim. Crime occurs in a spatial situation and has a temporal sequence which involves the particular act between offender and victim and the wider social context in which this occurs. To control crime from a realist perspective involves intervention at each part of the square of crime: at the level of the factors which give rise to the putative offender (such as structural unemployment), the informal system (such as lack of public mobilization), the victim (such as inadequate target hardening), and the formal system (such as ineffective policing). In realism all points of intervention are possible and necessary. Intervention based polemically on one mode alone, whether it is argued that, for instance, more jobs or public mobilization through neighbourhood watch, or the target hardening of buildings or more effective policing, may make some gains. But intervention on one level alone – even if effective – will inevitably have declining marginal gains. A multi-pronged strategy is always desirable for this reason alone, but all the more so in that each level of intervention interacts with the others. This being said, interventions at the level of social structure (such as changes in employment opportunities) are more effective than changes in the criminal justice system. A perfect criminal justice system operating to the letter of the rule of law would still disproportionately prosecute and incarcerate the poor. Realism would, of course, acknowledge that 'on the day', without – and to a lesser extent even with – long-term structural intervention, other interventions are necessary.

Realism prioritizes structural intervention, but it concedes that interventions at all levels, from target hardening to policing, are inevitably necessary. One cannot blame the crime rate on the inadequacies of the criminal justice system; one can criticize the rampant inefficiencies, malpractices and unfairness that abound within those institutions, and point to the way in which such unfairness adds fuel to the sense of social injustice that the offender has already experienced (Matza, 1964). But the causal push which creates crime originates primarily within the social structure, not within the administration of justice.

Realists, therefore, stress the primacy of intervention in the social structure over the interventions of the criminal justice system (CJS). They neither seek to elevate the CJS to a paramount role, nor to suggest that CJS interventions are irrelevant or inevitably counter-productive. Rather, they insist on the minimal use of the CJS while stressing its importance as the necessary body of coercively empowered institutions within a democracy which backs up informal and non-CJS institutions. For some commentators, on the right, the CJS is seen somewhat like a magic wand which, if waved more vigorously, will solve the problem of crime. For liberals, it is believed that if only the wand were waved in an impartial way, in time, with due process, the problems of crime would be greatly alleviated. And on the left, abolitionists – often, unsurprisingly, with a background in law – would seem to believe that if the wand ceased waving, crime itself would disappear and resolve itself into a series of rather minor 'problematic situations'. All of these notions are false. All evidence suggests that a more punitive response to crime is unproductive. Due process is an important goal to fight for, but it will not remedy the substantive inequalities within society which engender crime and generate the class and racial disproportions in our prisons. And, whereas one would wholeheartedly agree about the withdrawal of the CJS from minor 'problematic situations', there are far too many serious crimes which must be attended to with the use of coercive sanctions and many more which are, at present, unacted upon and neglected (cf. Hulsman, 1986).

Informal versus formal systems of control
It is a central finding of modern criminology that the criminal justice system has only a minor purchase on the overall crime rate. The rate of crime relates to changes in the social and economic structure on which the CJS has little effect.

Informal agencies of social control (the public, the family, the peer group) are the major method of controlling crime once it has occurred. A vital agency in this area is the strictures placed upon people by employment (Young, 1979). Non-policing formal agencies, such as the school or the everyday surveillance which occurs in shops, are also of great importance. The police and the CJS have a minor, yet vital, role in this process. In this, the police are largely dependent on public support in their efforts to control crime (see Kinsey et al., 1986) and the effect of the CJS is, in part, predicated upon the level at which public opinion backs up state stigmatization (Braithwaite, 1989).

Left idealism and the denial of the role of the CJS
A commonplace among left idealists and others of the abolitionist persuasion is to move from the recognition of the importance of non-penal methods of controlling crime, to discarding the CJS altogether. Louk Hulsman (1986) makes the 'discovery' that the vast majority of 'crimes' are not dealt with by the CJS. He moves from this to suggest the abolition of the CJS and, indeed, the abolition of the concept of crime altogether. For him 'crime has no ontological reality'. Crime is not the *object* but the *product* of criminal policy (p. 71). The informal system of control, which deals with the majority of 'problematic situations' should be extended to tackling their totality.

Of course, only a tiny proportion of events which are potentially criminal are, in fact, criminalized. In realist terms it is even more drastic than this: a near infinity of acts could be criminalized if criminal codes were interpreted with complete abandon. Criminalization involves the selection of certain activities in a political process which stretches from the public via the police through the courts. All of this is well documented by conventional analysis of the creation of criminal statistics (Lea and Young, 1984: ch. 1). What should be stresed is that this is not merely a top-down process, as social constructionists and left idealists would maintain, but involves a high level of grass roots public input. A large proportion of this process is based on public consensus, although there is inevitably, *as this is by necessity a political process*, argument at the edges of this consensus (for example controversy over cannabis; what or what is not pornographic; the comparative immunity of crimes of the powerful; definitions of rape, etc). That is, arguments about how the net of social control should be reduced and extended. For realists it is vital that such a process of criminalization should be democratized. It involves the public, but it does not involve the public enough. For example, that police priorities should fall in line with public priorities (Jones et al., 1986). Such a recognition of the importance of criminal law in the process of democratic social control does not imply that the existing sanctions and mechanisms are accepted uncritically. On the contrary, community alternatives to prison (Matthews, 1989), the use of mediation schemes (Matthews, 1988), the advocacy of non-criminal regulation where possible (Pearce, 1990) are all high on the agenda. Realists, however, that the use of criminal sanctions, albeit in a diminished fashion, is essential for the maintenance of social order and, indeed, as a back-up measure to strengthen the efficacy of informal modes of conflict resolution. The choice is not between informal or formal measures of control, nor do these measures parallel the distinction between non-coercive and coercive intervention. Informal sanctions can, of course, be more repressive than formal sanctions. Realists certainly do not criticize the repressive nature of much state control in order to replace this by the tyranny of public opinion. It is only by maintaining a balance between formal and informal sanctions that we can hope to reduce crime without descending to the totalitarian 'utopia' of the ubiquitous neighbourhood busybody and the omniscient intolerance of an 'other-directed' *Gemeinschaft*.

The police and crime

The argument that the police have little effect on the crime rate is curiously prevalent among criminologists of all parts of the political spectrum. It is held by administrative criminologists (Morris and Heal, 1981), by right realists such as Wilson (1975), who stress order maintenance rather than crime control as the prime police function, by left idealists who are certain that policing is about politics, not about crime (Bunyan, 1976), and even by sectors of the police themselves. Indeed, as Sir Peter Imbert, Commissioner of Police for the Metropolis, put it recently: 'Blaming police for the rise in crime is as absurd as blaming the fire brigade for the increase of fires.'

All of this reverses the conventional wisdom of the police as the front line in the fight against crime. We have reviewed these arguments extensively in *Losing the Fight against Crime* (Kinsey et al., 1986: ch. 4). Yet while realists firmly place the major motor which produces crime in society at large and emphasize the central role of the public and of the multi-agencies, we do not let the police off the hook. The assertion that the police have little effect in crime rates frequently blurs the issues because it (a) does not recognize that most research is about the marginal effects of extra police, not about the deterrent effect of existing police levels; (b) generalizes from correlations between specific crimes (such as burglary) and particular policing practices (such as beat policing) and the general crime rate (Crawford et al., 1990: ch. 7).

Once again the principle of specificity: the deterrent effect varies with the type of crime, the type of policing (if beat policing what *type* of beat policing?), the locality and the existing relationships between the public and relevant agencies. The deterrent effect of policing is dependent on public confidence; it can be high where public support is great (as in the suburbs) and break down in the inner city, where public confidence collapses. Conversely, the power of the informal system to control crime may be great if police back-up is present, but may be radically demoralized where the police are seen as an alien force. More police can have a deterrent effect or can reduce deterrence, dependent on the context. This stress on specificity simply does not allow us to marshal blancmange figures of police staff levels correlated with general clear-up rates. Nor is it admirable to move from particular police practices and specific crimes to assertions about the deterrent effect of policing in general. The most frequent research example involves generalizations based on beat policing (largely unspecified; is it aggressive patrols which alienate the public or user-friendly policing which gives public confidence?) and the burglary rates against which beat policing is scarcely likely to have any impact in the first place.

It has been suggested recently by Mathiesen (1990) that the realist project has placed all its faith in better policing as the major mode of controlling crime. It is difficult to imagine how such a caricature has been constructed: charitably one imagines it is due to restricted reading rather than limited scholarship. In particular, it involves generalization from texts that were concerned with the intervention over police accountability (Kinsey et al., 1986). It should be clear from this chapter that the control of crime involves interventions on all levels: on the social causes of crime, on social control exercised by the community and the formal agencies, and on the situation of the victim. Further-more, that social causation is given the highest priority, whereas formal agencies, such as the police, have a vital role, yet one which has in the conventional literature been greatly exaggerated. It is not the 'Thin Blue Line', but the social bricks and mortar of civil society which are the major bulwark against crime. Good jobs with a discernible future, housing estates that tenants can be proud of, community facilities which enhance a sense of cohesion and belonging, a reduction in unfair income inequalities, all create a society which is more cohesive and less criminogenic.

It is obvious from this analysis that certain crimes are more difficult to control than others (particularly if they are consensual and in private) and that particular points of intervention in the shape of the crime present greater difficulties than others. There are resistant points and there are weak spots. Both the type of intervention and what agency is involved must be tailored to these structures.

The principle of multi-agency intervention

Multi-agency intervention is the planned, coordinated response of the major social agencies to problems of crime and incivilities. The central reason for multi-agency social intervention is that of realism: it corresponds both to the realities of crime and to the realities of social control. Social control in industrial societies is, by its very nature, multi-agency. The problem is that it is not coordinated and represents a series of other disparate policy initiatives, with little overall rationale for the allocation of resources, and institutions which are often at loggerheads with each other. Yet, as I have discussed, the multi-agencies are mutually dependent on each other and each agency is dependent on public support, whether an agency dealing with domestic violence, child abuse or juvenile delinquency. In this section I wish to deal with the relationship between (a) the agencies and particular forms of crime; (b) the agencies and the public; (c) the agencies themselves.

The agencies and crime

Different agencies are involved for different crimes and at different stages in the process of tackling offenders If we compare burglary to child abuse we see immediately the differences between the involve-ment of the various agencies. Burglary will, in general, have a high police involvement in terms of the apprehension of the criminal. The local council, on the other hand, will have the greatest role in the 'target hardening' of the local estate. If the culprit is an adult, social services will be unlikely to be involved, but they will, of course, do so if the offender is a juvenile. For child abuse, in contrast, the social services will play a paramount role; the schools will be major insti-tutions of detection, and the medical profession will play an important role in terms of corroboration. And in terms of the different stages of tackling offenders: one can see how the police role as a back-up agency for providing coercive intervention where necessary and legal evidence in the courts occurs at different times in the procedure than the long-term process of social work intervention.

Different agencies are involved at different parts of the trajectory of the offender As we have seen, a realist approach to offenders sees the development of criminal behaviour over time. It breaks down this trajectory of offending into its component parts and notes how different agencies can and should be operative at different stages. Thus, to recapitulate these stages, we have: (1) the *background causes* of crime; (2) the *moral context* of opting for criminal behaviour; (3) the *situation of committing* crime; (4) the *detection of crime*; (5) the *response to the offender*; (6) the *response to the victim*. Let us examine these one by one, noting the factors involved and the agencies with the power to intervene.

Background causes These lie in relative deprivation as witnessed in poverty and unemployment, in overcrowded housing conditions, in poor leisure facilities and in inadequately funded families (particularly single parent). Here central government, the local authorities, and local business have responsibility.

The moral context   Here we have in particular the family, the education system, the mass media, youth organizations and religious organizations. Here the public themselves, the councils, in their provision of education and youth facilities, the media professional in the context of the often heavy media, of adolescents, and local religious and youth leaders, have their roles.

The situation of commission   Here target hardening, lighting, public willingness to intervene and police patrols, are important. Thus the important agencies are the council, the police and the public themselves.

The detection of crime   Here, as discussed above, the cooperation of police and public is paramount, both in terms of informing the police and witnessing in courts.

The response to the offender   Here the role of the police and the courts is paramount in their dual aim of punishment and rehabilitation. A rehabilitated offender, of course, should not be a recidivist. Here social services are prominent in their role of caring for young people, but also in terms of possibilities of employment, and the shoring up of unstable family situations.

The response to the victim   Up to now I have discussed the whole process of multi-agency social intervention as if it was just concerned with dealing with offenders and preventing offences. We must never forget, however, the other half of the dyad of crime: the victim. Here again, it is obvious that various agencies must be involved in tackling the problem of criminal victimization. Social services, for example, may have to deal with the after-effects of a mugging of an elderly person, the council has to repair doors after burglary, battered women's refuges have to deal with domestic violence, the police have to deal with the victims' fear on the spot. Victim Support has a vital role to play throughout. Thus our measurement of success – or failure for that matter – is not solely in terms of the levels of offending (that is, crime), but in the levels of victim support provided.

I have discussed the wide range of tasks which influence crime, which involve different agencies and which are influential at different times in the trajectory of offending. It is important to note how these agencies have different material possibilities of intervening and act within given political limits. We have to choose, then, what agencies are involved and what factors can feasibly be manipulated.

Our approach then views crime as a developing system, from its initial causes to the impact on the victim. In doing this it places the responsibility for crime control on a wide range of agencies and the public themselves.

Multi-agencies and the public

The literature on multi-agency intervention is dominated by a discussion of the relationship between the institutions involved. This analysis, quite correctly, focuses on the possibilities of cooperation and likely conflicts between the agencies. It omits, however, a crucial link in the scheme, namely the relationship between the agencies and the public. I have noted the vital role which the public plays in policing. The recognition of this is, if anything, a major part of modern criminological thinking. And we must not restrict our attention to police–public relations, but the relationships between the public and the various agencies concerned with crime control. For the social services, education, probation and the local council, no less than the police, are dependent on public cooperation.

Relationship between agencies

The democratic relationship between agencies must be based on their specialist knowledge and purchase on particular crimes. That is a division of labour predicated on the specific segment of the crime process in which the agency specializes. For example, at what point in time along the continuum of the development of crime, outlined above, is a particular agency's involvement paramount and what perspective does the agency represent? In the latter instance, a juvenile delinquent, for example, may be regarded from the point of view of whether guilty or not by the police, the context of a family with problems by the social services, and as part of a family which causes problems for others in the estate by the housing officers. There has to be pre-agreed consensus as to specialism, although in some cases more than one agency will be involved at the same point. Lighting, for example, will be under the auspices of both the local authority's architects' department and their housing officers. Different crimes will, of course, involve different multi-agency cooperation. Child abuse will involve a strong medical involvement, as well as police and social services. Domestic violence will involve the voluntary agencies as well as the more usual constituents.

Having brought together these agencies there will, despite an agreement on acknowledged specialisms, be a necessary conflict of interests. In child abuse, for example, social work will, by necessity of its brief, focus on the general welfare of the child within the family; the police more on the actual issues of culpability; the paediatrician on the extent of physical contact and harm. What is necessary, in the coordination of such expertise, is that in the final analysis a corporate decision be made, after listening to the contributions of each agency, and backed with sufficient executive power to come to an agreed decision. As it is, the agencies discuss together, yet then too often merely proceed upon their own paths with their own agenda. Such imbalances are dramatically seen where, in the case of child abuse, either medical or social services play too dominant a role, or, in the case of crime prevention, where the police take too prominent a role. It is the role of local authorities to provide this coordinating role. It is the ultimate task of national government to ascertain how the funding of resources to each agency is based on the actual cost-effective contribution of each part, rather than, as at present, allow resources to be decided by the separate agencies themselves. Such a conception of minimal policing in the context of multi-social intervention has clear implications for the second dimension of our analysis. Here there is widespread community support for such a proposal (Painter et al., 1989). It does not involve a domination by the police on the multiple agencies, and, though advocating cooperation between the agencies, it does not suggest a corporatism involving a cosy level of agreement. Rather, because of the different approaches and priorities of each agency, room has to be made for a healthy debate and conflict of perspectives within a consensus delineated by public demands for the control of specific areas (cf. Sampson et al., 1985). Finally, in terms of the second dimension, the public accountability of agencies – a concern hitherto largely omitted in discussion of multi-agency intervention – the priority is to ensure efficiency and the need for public bodies to fall in line with the demands of the public whose support is necessary for their effectiveness and who, out of their rates and taxes, pay these bodies for the task of achieving a reasonable level of community safety. All of this, with due regard to the three dimensions of multi-agency intervention, suggests the basis for a restructuring of these institutions so as to ensure a maximum level of service delivery in this area, while protecting the rights and dignity of the offender.

The principle of rational democratic input

Taking people seriously

The public pay for community safety; they ultimately empower the police and the local authority to make provisions for a safe environment. There is much talk, at the moment, of the quality of life, and the emergence of green issues as priorities in the platforms of all political parties. Considerable focus is given, quite correctly, to architecture, to consumer satisfaction, to creating an environment in the city which makes it a pleasure to live in. But what can be more central to the quality of life than the ability to walk down the street at night without

...ar, to feel safe in one's home, to be free from harassment and incivilities in the day-to-day experience of urban life?

The social survey is a democratic instrument: it provides a reasonably accurate appraisal of people's fears and of their experience of victimization. Local surveys further allow us to move beyond the abstraction of aggregate national statistics. Crime is extremely geographically focused and policing varies widely between the suburbs and the inner city. To add the crime rates for a suburban area to that of an inner-city area produces blancmange figures of little use to anyone. More invidiously, it allows politicians to talk of irrational fears of crime when compared to the actual risk rate of the 'average' citizen. The 1982 *British Crime Survey* showed that the risk of experiencing a robbery in England and Wales was once every five centuries; an assault resulting in injury, once every century; a family car stolen, once every 60 years and a burglary once every 50 years (Hough and Mayhew, 1983). But crime is extensively geographically focused and 'irrational' fears become the more rational with geographical focus on the inner city. And the often-made assertion that certain groups have an irrational fear of crime because of their supposedly low risk rates often disappears on closer examination. Ascribing irrationality to women, for example, is based on ignoring that much crime against women, such as domestic violence, is concealed in the official figures, that women are less tolerant of violence than men and that they experience harassment on a level which is unknown to most men. The latter point, particularly, is important for policing public areas. Women experience a wider spectrum of crime than men. Their range of victimization extends from harassment to serious crime. The range for men is more likely to be experienced in the more serious end of the spectrum. Because of this, men find it difficult to comprehend women's fears. The equivalent experience of sexual harassment for men would be if every time they walked out of doors they were met with catcalls asking if they would like a fight. And the spectrum which women experience is all the more troublesome in that each of the minor incivilities could escalate to more serious violence. Sexual harassment could be a prelude to attempted rape; domestic verbal quarrels could trigger off domestic violence; burglary is feared, not only as a property crime, but as a possible precursor to sexual assault. If crime deteriorates the quality of life for men, it has a much more dramatic impact on the lives of women in the inner city.

Social surveys, therefore, allow us to give voice to the experience of people, and they enable us to differentiate the safety needs of different sectors of the community. In this they often make reasonable the supposedly irrational. But it must not be thought that irrationality does not occur with regard to crime and the means of its control. Crime is a prime site of social anxiety and the mass media provide the citizen with an extraordinary, everyday diet of spectacular crimes, often of the most statistically atypical kind. It is, perhaps, not surprising that the news value of the most unusual garish offences is higher than that of the more mundane crimes that daily plague the lives of the inner-city dweller. And in a free society there is little that can, or should, be done about such media predilections. For in a real sense the most unusual examples of inhumanity tell us something of the extremes of moral depravity that are possible in today's society. The trouble occurs when the citizen comes to believe that what is typical on television is typical in his or her neighbourhood. The debate on the effects of the mass media on public attitudes is long, fraught and, in part, unresolved (Cohen and Young, 1981). What is a useful rule of thumb, however, is that the mass media have greatest influence on opinion where people have little direct knowledge of the matter in question and the least where they have direct empirical experience. Applying this to the repeated findings of victimization studies, we would expect that there is little chance of inner-city dwellers being particularly irrational about most of the common serious crimes.

When we turn to crime control, the possibility of public irrationality is considerably greater. For, although they may have experienced victimization, they have, on the whole, little knowledge as to how effective crime control occurs. It comes as a surprise, for example, that a large proportion of serious crime is solved by the public rather than by police investigation. And, as we have seen, neighbourhood watch is widely seen as a panacea for burglary, despite being largely ineffective.

Social surveys can, therefore, provide us with a democratic input into the direction and prioritization of crime control. But they cannot provide us with a blueprint. You cannot read policy directives from social surveys but neither can you provide directives without a real consumer input. The victimization survey accurately provides a map of the problems of an area. Although based on public input, it delivers what any individual member of the public is ignorant of: that is how private problems are publicly distributed. In this task, it pinpoints which social groups within the population face the greatest risk rates and geographically pinpoints where these occurrences most frequently occur. In this it directs crime intervention initiatives towards these people and places which are most at risk. It therefore reveals the concealed crime rate and it ascertains its social and spatial focus. But it goes beyond this, for risk rates alone, however delineated, do not measure the true impact of crime and hence the actual patterning of crime as a social problem. To do this we must advance beyond the one-dimensional approach of aggregate risk rates and place crime in its social context. The myth of the equal victim underscores much of conventional victimology with its notion that victims are, as it were, equal billiard balls, and the risk rate involves merely the calculation of the changes of an offending billiard ball impacting upon them. People are, of course, not equal; they are, more or less, vulnerable, depending on their place in society. First of all, at certain parts of the social structure, we have a compounding of social problems.

If we were to draw a map of the city outlining areas of high infant mortality, bad housing, unemployment, poor nutrition, etc, we would find that all these maps would coincide and that further, the outline traced would correspond to those areas of high criminal victimization (Clarke, 1980). And those suffering from street crime would also suffer most from white-collar and corporate crime (Lea and Young, 1984). Further, this compounding of social problems occurs against those who are more or less vulnerable because of their position in the social structure. That is, people who have least power socially suffer most from crime. Most relevant here is the social relationships of age, class, gender and race. Realist analysis, by focusing on the combination of these fundamental social relationships, allows us to note the extraordinary differences between social groups as to both the impact of crime and the focus of policing. It is high time, therefore, that we substituted *impact* statistics for *risk* statistics.

The principle of rational democratic output

Let us now turn to outcome. At first this would seem obvious: the *modus vivendi* of crime control is to control crime. But we must ask: what crimes are being controlled, at what cost, and where do these crimes figure in public priorities? That is, we must connect up demand with supply; what crimes the public prioritize in terms of community safety and how effective the various agencies and initiatives are at their control with an eye to cost-effectiveness. But efficiency alone is an insufficient indicator of success. It is quite possible to pour resources into a particular estate or area to good result. But the reduction of crime at a particular point in the city may have little effect on the overall crime rate. At its most acute, the individual citizen may turn his or her home into a veritable fortress of locks, bolts and guard dogs, which will undoubtedly reduce the chances of crime at a particular point in a street, but not reduce – indeed, may increase – the incidence of crime in adjacent properties. Or, on a larger scale, residents of a private estate may employ their own security guards and, by environmental means, isolate their housing from the neighbourhood. Such social sanitization may greatly reduce the incidence of crime in such privatized areas. Or, within the public realm, a local authority may select an estate and implement considerable degrees of target hardening on doors and windows, coupled with an expensive concierge system. Such 'show casing' of one estate may produce good particular results, but have little effect on the universal incidence of crime in the area. The task of an effective crime policy is to reduce crime in general. In this it is like a community health project; success is not measured by the extent to which the well-off can purchase vaccines, private health care and medicines, but the degree to which such indicators as the levels of infectious diseases are reduced, infant mortality in general curtailed, overall lifespan increased, etc.

Crime, like illness, is a universal problem. It affects all classes, ages, races; men and women. For this reason, being a prevalent and universal phenomenon, it rates very highly in people's assessment of problems of their area. More people, for example, see crime in an inner-city area such as the London Borough of Islington as a problem than they do unemployment, housing or education. This is because these latter problems, however serious, affect, most directly, only parts of the population: those who are unemployed, those with poor housing, those with children at school. But however universal a problem crime is, it affects particular parts of the population to a greater extent than others. In part, this is because the incidence of crime focuses on certain parts of the population rather than others, but also, most importantly, because the impact of identical crimes varies considerably with the vulnerability of those who are the targets of crime. To this extent, we must not only seek to reduce the crime rate universally, but we must allocate greater resources to those who suffer the most. Once again, community health provides a model. Ill-health is a universal human problem, but ill-health focuses more on certain sectors of the population than it does on others. We must, therefore, in order to reduce the general rate of crime, target our resources. Unfortunately, and this has been a general problem of welfare provision, resources are not distributed so much to those in greatest need, as to those with the greater political muscle and social persuasion. The history of the National Health Service and of state educational provisions has adequately displayed this. And, as I have argued, crime control has its parallel problems in the shape of the privatization of community safety and the 'show casing' of selected areas of public housing.

The interrelated nature of intervention
The degree of impact of an intervention about crime by one agency is dependent on the other agencies. To take a simple example: no amount of propagation by the police of crime prevention advice in terms of better locks and bolts will be effective on estates if the council does not simultaneously strengthen the doorframes of its tenants' houses. Or, of greater significance, police effectiveness is almost totally predicated on

public support – it cannot function without the information flow from the informal system of social control. And the same is true of deterrence: the effect of police cautioning or sentences of the control relates closely to the degree of public stigma. That is, we must concern ourselves, not only with how effective each piece is with regard to crime control, but how these various pieces can be welded into an effective mutually supporting intervention. As an effective strategy in one agency will need support from other institutions, we can only judge the effectiveness of an innovation in practice in one area to the extent that the requisite support occurs elsewhere.

Realism about cost effectiveness in tackling crime   Realism states that any intervention has its costs. Different crime control measures have to be measured against: (a) how effective are they compared to each other? (b) how effective is the marginal increase in resources in one area rather than another? (c) what is the cost of the measure in terms of other desiderata, for example, the quality of life or the exercise of civil liberties?

Our point should now be clear. A realist policy acknowledges that there are various methods which, if properly tested, monitored and costed, can reduce crime. But any one method, however effective, will have declining marginal returns if taken too far and too exclusively. Furthermore, any one method, be it public surveillance through neighbourhood watch, extra police on the streets, or target hardening, will have costs which impact on the quality of life and the freedom of citizens. Present government policy, by putting too great an emphasis on target hardening and ignoring the conditions which give rise to crime, has created an imbalance in intervention. It has focused on reducing the opportunities for crime, not on its causes, on one half of the equation rather than on both of its sides.

Every social intervention inevitably has unintended repercussions. The cost of crime control has to be measured against the degree of displacement of crime occurring and the effect on the quality of life (from the aesthetics of target hardening to the civil liberties aspect of intensive policing). An effective intervention will have a crime displacement which is quantifiably lower, qualitatively of a less serious nature which directs crime away from the most vulnerable social groups (in the area of drug control, see Dorn and South, 1987). Its social cost will have to be weighed against any losses in the quality of life. Realistically, we have to decide politically what level of crime is tolerable when weighed against such social costs. No method of crime control will be totally effective: we must talk in terms of palpable gains rather than magical solutions.

Open and closed systems   The distinction between open and closed systems is a fundamental distinction made in the recent realist philosophy of science (Bhaskar, 1980). Most scientific laws are predicated on research carried out *in vitro*, that is closed systems, where all extraneous factors are held constant. Here causality can be traced with a degree of simplicity. But in the actual natural world, for example, in sciences such as meteorology, the degree of extraneous factors present in an open system make statement of cause and effect extremely difficult. *X* follows *Y*, depending on the contingency of circumstance: it is better, therefore, to speak of 'causal powers' which may or may not be enacted, depending on circumstance. The social world is an 'open system' *par excellence*.

To hold that an intervention in policing or other forms of crime control, in such an open system, would be instrumental in changing the crime rate begs a series of questions: namely, that the number of possible victims, offenders and public reaction to crime are constant. But changes in the social structure of the area affect all of these factors. For example:

1 increased gentrification would affect the number of victims and also by increasing relative deprivation, the number of putative offenders;
2 increased population mobility would affect the social solidarity of the area and hence the strength of public control of crime;
3 changes in the age structure, particularly of young males, would affect the number of putative offenders;
4 changes in employment and economic marginalization would affect the number of offenders;

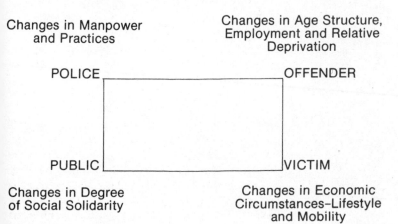

Changes in Manpower and Practices

Changes in Age Structure, Employment and Relative Deprivation

POLICE — OFFENDER

PUBLIC — VICTIM

Changes in Degree of Social Solidarity

Changes in Economic Circumstances–Lifestyle and Mobility

Figure 2.3

5   changes in lifestyle by increasing, for example, the number of evenings out made by members of the public would affect the victimization rate, both in terms of risks in public space and the risks of homes unattended.

We can attempt to control for some of these, but an open system over any reasonable length of time will exhibit the movement of many of these factors. What I am pointing to is that the process which gives results to crime rates is a system of relationships, and what is more, it is an open system (see Figure 2.3).

The implication of such an open system is that – with the exception of short-term experiments, where a social intervention such as improvements in lighting is introduced and the effects measured (Painter, 1989) – it is extremely difficult to pinpoint cause and effect.

The principle of democratic measurement

Realism and the criminal statistics

The problem of criminal statistics is the base-line problem of criminology. It is a recognized problem which has a history as long as the discipline, stretching back to the work of Alphonse Quetelet in the 1830s. It is a concern which has haunted every theory. For if the problem of what causes crime is a conundrum, the difficulty of knowing, in the first place, what crimes occur, to what extent and where, undercuts all others. It is on the shifting sand of the statistics that the most elaborate and powerful structures of theory flounder.

The problem comes down to answering the question of what is the 'real' rate of crime and, indeed, is there such an entity? Let us dispose first of the notion that victimization studies technically solve this question by overcoming the problem of the 'dark figure'. For, despite grandiose claims for victimization data (Sparks et al., 1977), all of the old problems remain, albeit in a less marked form. Victimization studies have dark figures, they are a product of research units whose conceptualization of the data from the questionnaire to the coding reflects their own values, and they ask questions of interviewees with different definitions of what constitutes a crime (Young, 1988b).

Realism propounds that rates of crime are by definition a result of the interplay of actors and reactors: of victims and offenders, on one hand, and of formal and informal control, on the other. Rates of crime change as these interacting sectors change and any satisfactory theory of crime must take cognizance of the totality of this process. The rate of crime is the result of a dynamic process of decision making, not a fixed datum 'out there' (Wheeler, 1967; Wilkins, 1964).

The simple belief that the crime rate is a gauge of offenders is wrong.

The crime rate goes up, it is true, when there are more motivated offenders: but it also goes up when there are more available victims or when the police and public are more lax in their control), or more sensitive in their definition of 'intolerable' behaviour. But how does the crime rate relate to the crime statistics? How does one move from infractions in the world to tabulated data on official reports? The crime rate is not a 'natural' act, crime rates do not spring automatically out of aggregates of illegalities. Someone has to embark on an act of collecting these varied, moral infractions together. Crime rates are not naturally and automatically produced phenomena, they are second order data produced by bureaucracies: whether the police, victimization survey work or criminologists engaged in self-report studies. They involve applying a fairly consistent measuring rod (such as have you been burgled/assaulted?) to a series of actions which the public inconsistently evaluates (holding differing definitions of what constitutes burglary/assault).

Crime is, by its very nature, a product of action and reaction. It involves behaviour and the variable legal response to that behaviour: an infraction and an evaluation. Criminal statistics, whether official, self-report, or victim report are, therefore, neither an objective fact of behaviour (Eysenck and Gudjonsson, 1989), nor merely a social construction dependent on the evaluation of the powerful. Different groups within society and different societies at various parts of historical time vary in their definitions of what is tolerable behaviour. The statistics of violence, as we have seen, depend on the extent of violent behaviour and the tolerance level to violence. There is no objective yardstick for crime, but a series of measuring rods dependent on the social group in which they are based. All societies and social groups, however, stigmatize a wide range of usurpation of the person and of property. At any point in time, various social groups will agree up to a point, then differ from that point onward. The measuring rod is not – and cannot be – consensual in an absolute sense, but it has a considerable overlap of agreement (Young, 1988b). All groups, for example, abhor violence against women, but they will vary in their definition of what constitutes abhorrent violence. For this reason, criminal statistics are, by their very nature, blurred; they can never be stated with precision, although they can be more or less democratically ascertained and can make possible a real, if hazy, outline of the constraints of the problem.

The comparison of crime rates between different groups, between different countries, and over time, is, therefore, a process by which we must be clearly aware of differences in value. The so-called 'education effect', where, for example, middle-class women claim higher rates of violence than working-class women, is a case in question (Sparks,

1981). It is not, however, beyond the capabilities of researchers to ask questions on not only reported violent behaviour and to construct tolerance scales towards violence. Furthermore, there is a level of specificity here, where certain crimes, such as burglary, have less of a subjective component than does violence (Hough, 1986). But even such 'objective' crimes have clear definitional variations: note the problems in international comparisons which often blur attempted burglaries with successful break-ins. Over time, in longitudinal studies, we must be aware that a 'successful' intervention, say a housing estate which reduces the behavioural manifestations of vandalism, may result in an increased intolerance to vandalism. Because of this, the resulting post-intervention survey may indicate more acts of vandalism than before or, even more puzzlingly, because of a decrease in behaviour concomitant with an increase in intolerance, no 'change' whatsoever (Young, 1988b).

If Quetelet pointed to the existence of a dark figure of crime, realist and feminist studies have pointed to how this dark figure is qualitatively structured. The dark figure varies with what type of crime committed by whom against which victim. Such an analysis takes us one step further. The dark figure expands and contracts with the values we bring to our study: recent studies of the extent of marital rape or changes in child abuse over time clearly indicate this.

Crime as a unifier

Both radical critics of the left and the right suggest that law and order is an issue which splits the community. For left idealists (Bridges et al., 1987), it involves the mobilization of state (and particularly police) definitions of crime with anti-working class and racist undertones. For the radical right, law and order is about the protection of the law-abiding from a predatory underclass. Realism sees the issue of crime as a major unifier: law and order, like health and education, are areas which affect the majority of the population, which is the constituency of social democratic politics (cf. Brown and Hogg, 1992). Right-wing law and order politics not only seek to divide the population, they are ineffective at controlling crime and would seek to privatize community safety – just as in health and education – in a fashion which would privilege the wealthy and the powerful. Furthermore, the poor suffer most from crime and, once again, as in health and education, have a priority of needs in social democratic policy. Crime is endemic throughout society, it is not a monopoly product of an underclass, although conventional crime is most endemic in the lower part of the class structure. And it is the poorer and most vulnerable sections of the population (less well-off whites, blacks, lower working-class women) against whom crimes of the powerful (from corporate crime, through

·lack of safety regulations, to police malpractices) and conventional crimes create the greatest impact. It is not an either/or between corporate crime and conventional crime as left idealists would maintain.

There is a widespread consensus throughout society of the importance of crime as an issue and the priority crimes to tackle. Certainly there are differences in emphasis between social groups, but research shows a consistent unity of concern, particularly with regard to crimes of violence and serious property offences (Jones et al., 1986). To point to a degree of consensus within the population about the definitions of various crimes is not to seek an absolute consensus. Indeed, in realist terms, this is impossible. But the unity of interest allows us the possibility, both of a common measuring rod, and a political base which can argue for taking crime seriously.

The principle of theory and practice

The problem goes something like this: intellectual and academic life in general and in the social sciences in particular, thrives best and depends upon a spirit of scepticism, doubt and uncertainty. Answers are provisional; thought is ambiguous; irony is deliberate. All this can best be achieved when one is free from pressures of everyday demands – especially those to be 'relevant' and to fit and tailor your ideas to serve the managers of society. Uncompromising intellectual honesty does not usually please politicians and civil servants.

Political life, on the other hand – and in this context I include social policy, welfare, social work, social control, criminal justice – calls for some immediate commitments. Decisions have to be made, clear public statements made, bets placed, budgets drawn up, doubts temporarily laid aside. You have to respond to values that are binding and encourage neither scepticism nor irony: social justice, humanitarianism, doing good, equality, citizenship, public safety, the needs of victims. All this familiar. But the familiar is always with us. (Cohen, 1990: 10–11)

The 'interior' history of an academic discipline involves the development of intellectual traditions, each with its own problematic and involving material problems of funding and employment. The 'exterior' history involves the political context, the policy problems of the outside world, and the various prevalent social and political ideologies (Hacking, 1981; Phipps, 1987; Young, 1988). The history of criminology may be written as an interior dialogue of ideas and debates, but it exists always in an exterior world of changing problems of crime and penality, of funding from central and local government agencies, of contemporary conceptions of human nature and social order. Theories of society do not come into being out of the blue. They arise out of the hunches and intuitions of people trying to make sense of the world around them: they arise out of real problems facing people in the social world which confronts them. The academic refines, develops and systemizes theory, but the agenda is set for him or her by the actual problems of the world outside the ivory tower and the text is largely pre-written by the social currents and fashions of the time. Whatever textbooks write about the 'interior' history of a discipline, as if it developed as the accumulated wisdom of the free exchange of ideas and criticism, the 'exterior' history of a subject, engendered by the practical problems of the outside world is, in fact, paramount.

The exterior world always penetrates the academic interior, whether it involves the most armchair radical theorist or the establishment criminologist working as a civil servant for a government bureaucracy. But, paradoxically, all are cocooned from reality by their social distance from their subjects, their obdurate preconceptions and myopia and, above all, by their political impotence. It is my contention that the achievement of a creative relationship between the interior and exterior worlds is essential to a mature criminology, albeit that it creates many dangers and pitfalls.

Theory is divorced from practice: theoreticians are divorced not just from practitioners, but from those who are the objects of their study. This is particularly true in criminology; criminologists live in different areas than criminals, they work in an academic milieu: the world of street crime or corporate crime, for that matter, is socially distant from them. They share little sympathy for the cop on the beat, they have a culture which is instinctively suspicious of both the bureaucrat in the town hall and the politician. Yet if we are to engage in a subcultural analysis of the police officer, the victim, the offender and the various publics constituting society, we cannot spare the criminologist from subcultural scrutiny. The fifth point in the square of crime is the criminologist (see Ruggiero, Chapter 5). A reflexive sociology must ground the academic in his or her milieu. As Gouldner put it:

> If every social theory is thus a tacit theory of politics, every theory is also a personal theory, inevitably expressing, coping and infused with the personal experience of the individuals who author it. Every social theory has both political and personal relevance which, according to the technical causes of social theory, it is not supposed to have. Consequently, both the man (sic) and his politics are of presumably 'autonomous' social theory.
>
> Yet, however disguised, an appreciable part of any sociological enterprise devolves from the sociologist's effort to explore, to objectify, and to universalize some of his own most deeply personal experiences. Much of any man's (sic) effort to know the social world around him is prompted by an effort, more or less disguised or deliberate, to know things that are personally important to him; which is to say, he aims at knowing himself and the experiences he has had in his social world (his relationship to it), and at changing this relationship in some manner. Like it or not, and know

it or not, in confronting the social world the theorist is also confronting himself....

> Whatever their other differences, all sociologists seek to study something in the social world that they take to be real; and, whatever their philosophy of science, they seek to explain it in terms of something that they feel to be real. Like other men (sic), sociologists impute reality to certain things in their social world. This is to say, they believe, sometimes with focal and sometimes only with subsidiary awareness, that certain things are truly attributable to the social world. In important part, their conception of what is 'real' derives from the domain assumptions they have learned in their culture. These culturally standardized assumptions are, however, differentiated by personal experience in different parts of the social structure. Individually accented by particular sentiment-generating experiences, the common domain assumptions in time assume personal arrangements; they become part of a man's personal reality. (1971: 40–41)

In this vein C. Wright Mills documents the underlying assumptions of small town society which textbooks of this period carried. Such domain assumptions involve preconceptions and blindness. The root of partiality: the emphasis upon only one part of the explanation in crime is both culturally and materially based. The classic example is that pointed to by David Matza:

> The scholar's or scientist's way of becoming partially blind is, inadvertently perhaps, to structure fields of injury in such a way as to obscure obvious connections or to take the connections for granted and leave the matter at that. The great task of disconnection – it was arduous and time-consuming – fell to the positive school of criminology. Among their most notable accomplishments, the criminological positivists succeeded in what would seem the impossible. They separated the study of crime from the workings and theory of the state. That done, and the lesson extended to deviation generally, the agenda for research and scholarship for the next half-century was relatively clear, especially with regard to what would *not* be studied. (1969: 143)

It is extraordinary that establishment criminologists who are the most politically constrained in their work can view themselves as politically neutral scientists *par excellence*. But radicals, as well, carry with them preconceptions and blindness. Their culture of scepticism, so rightly prized, is sceptical only in certain areas: it is naive in others. What are we to make of the arch-sceptic Michel Foucault when he comments:

> At the end of the eighteenth century, people dreamed of a society without crime. And then the dream evaporated. Crime was too useful for them to dream of anything as crazy – or ultimately as dangerous – as a society without crime. No crime means no police. What makes the presence and control of the police tolerable for the population, if not fear of the criminal? This institution of the police, which is so recent and so oppressive, is only justified by that fear. If we accept the presence in our midst of these

uniformed men, who have the exclusive right to carry arms, who demand our papers, who come and prowl on our doorsteps, how would any of this be possible if there were no criminals? And if there weren't articles every day in the newspapers telling us how numerous and dangerous our criminals are? (1980: 7)

There are, as Edward Thompson remarked about left idealist positions on law and order 'In secure and secluded places, some marvellously abstract notions afloat' (1980: 173). And political conceptions tacitly held are reinforced by the social distance of the criminologist from his or her subject matter. It is this social distance which was largely to account for the 'great denial' of the rise of crime among liberal criminologists in the late 1960s and early 1970s, which makes it difficult for male academics to understand the problem of crime and sexual harassment for women, and which was the moving force in the realist argument against both administrative criminology and left idealism. And the underestimation of the problem of crime by the latter criminologies became, of course, the basis for the initial slogan of realist criminology: to take people and crime seriously.

The bridge between the academic milieu and the deviant is constructed in two ways by research and, more rarely, by involvement in practical interventions. It is here that preconceptions should alter and myopia become unblinkered. But the material and cultural limitations are difficult to shake off and often not recognized. Research demands funding, seldom are there no strings attached, particularly if the researcher wishes the contracts to be renewed. Grants, like lunches, are seldom free. In all western countries the major research funding is central government, and this alone severely structures preconceptions and blindness (Young, 1988c). Radical sources of funding exhibit precisely the same problems. Taboo issues such as race and crime are systematically ignored by the liberal establishment (Wilbanks, 1985).

Both quantitative and qualitative research frequently involves a *projection* of the researcher's preconceptions on interviewees. Crime surveys, for example, typically provide a questionnaire menu of options which simply do not correspond to the lived experience of those interviewed. The modal type of crime for a middle-class male, for example, is the burglary: this generates a discrete 'event-orientation' which fails to encompass 'incessant' violence experienced by lower working-class groups (Genn, 1988), the continuous nature of domestic violence (Mooney, 1991) or the spectrum of harassment experienced by women in public spaces and working-class Asians in inner-city housing estates. Yet the 'bridge' between theory and data, for quantitative researchers, is regularly experienced as a row of figures on a computer printout: a small army of interviewers shielding the preconceptions of the theorist. Qualitative research, much heralded as being more intimate and reflexive, frequently involves a simple projection of the researcher's preconceptions. Margaret Mead was not alone in being deceived and deceiving herself. Stan Cohen, in his introduction to the revised edition of *Folk Devils and Moral Panics* (1980), trenchantly notes how radical ethnographers frequently treat subcultures like Rorschach blots.

If empirical research frequently involves the projection of preconceptions on its subject matter, criminological practice displays a welter of unmonitored projection. If there is anything one can agree with in the work of Wilson it is his dictum: 'Above all we can try to learn more about what works and in the process abandon our ideological preconceptions about what *ought* to work.' It must be said, however, that Wilson, in a typical act of inversion and partiality, ushers one set of ideological preconceptions out of the door simply to make room for another. But the dictum remains true; put simply: politicians of all persuasions throw money at crime problems. Millions of pounds, dollars and yen are spent every year on crime prevention with scarcely a thought as to cost effectiveness. Monitored research is rare and is, as I have argued, much more difficult than is usually acknowledged. Most practice is divorced from theory on all but a rudimentary level. A considerable part of criminological theory is, in fact, the critique by armchair theorists of other people's practice. To an extent this is a necessary and vital intervention. For if theoreticians, in their research, constantly face the problem of substantiating their preconceptions, practitioners within their own ideological and material context have a pronounced tendency to self-congratulation. As Dennis Rosenbaum notes in his exhaustive and meticulous examination of community crime prevention programmes:

> Despite all the impressive statistics and laudatory accomplishments attributed to community prevention programs, the standard evaluations in this field, which structure the foundation of public opinion about the success of these programs are seriously wanting.

> The endorsement of community crime prevention programs extends from many quarters, including federal state and local government agencies as well as community organizations. The enthusiastic embracing of community crime prevention is perhaps most apparent at the grass-root level, where practitioners acclaim the utility of their efforts through popular press articles and numerous homespun program publications, newsletters, and guidebooks that also serve to assist interested communities in the planning and implementation of programs.

> Not everyone has the same level of interest in presenting the 'hard facts'. To obtain program funding from public or private sources, grant applications often have a strong motivation to convince the funding agency that it will be investing in a proven, highly effective program for preventing crime in their

community. Likewise, the granting agencies, although wanting to remain neutral in the absence of hard data, also want to believe that they were supporting a good 'product'. Moreover, the media are very interested in success stories inasmuch as our losses in the seventeen-year 'war against crime' have greatly outnumbered our victories. Consequently, we have witnessed literally hundreds of media stories about the proven successes of community crime prevention over the past decade. Given this state of affairs, the primary 'checks and balances' must come from the academic community, armed with evaluation research skills and disinterested in the direction of the outcome. (1986: 19, 22, 23).

And, of course, Rosenbaum is talking about US research, where he can find less than 20 satisfactory monitored pieces of intervention. In Britain the situation is much bleaker – most community crime prevention programmes are simply not monitored, or if they are, are monitored using patently inadequate data and measures of success and failure.

Theory and practice are, thus, both our subjects of investigation. They both belong to the orbit of criminology.

Conclusion: the scope of criminology

The problem which faces criminology is not insignificant, however, and, arguably, its dilemma is even more fundamental than that facing sociology. The whole *raison d'être* of criminology is that it addresses crime. It categorizes a vast range of activities and treats them as if they were all subject to the same laws – whether laws of human behaviour, genetic inheritance, economic rationality, development or the like. The argument within criminology has always been between those who give primacy to one form of explanation rather than another. The thing that criminology cannot do is deconstruct crime. It cannot locate rape or child sexual abuse in the domain of sexuality or theft in the domain of economic activity or drug use in the domain of health. To do so would be to abandon criminology to sociology; but more importantly it would involve abandoning the idea of a unified problem which requires a unified response – at least, at the theoretical level. However, left realist criminology does not seem prepared for this. (Smart, 1990: 77)

Good criminology, of course, does precisely this: relate rape or child sexual abuse to the domain of sexuality, theft to the domain of economic activity, and drug use to the domain of health. But neither can the sociology of sexuality, economics or health studies remain within their watertight domains. Good work in these areas rarely does. But what Smart would seem to argue is that the domain of criminology should be cut up and disposed of between the various, more fundamental domains. Because it addresses a series of disparate behaviours? Is this not true of the domains of sexuality, economics and health? Illicit drug use is an economic activity, it is a health problem and, in the case of certain drugs, it has clear sexual connotations. To which domain should we reduce our studies? But enough of such demarcation disputes. Realist criminology starts from the deconstruction of the criminal act into its fundamental components: law and state agencies, the public and various institutions of civil societies, the victim and the offender. This is the domain of criminology. It is these formal relationships – which encompass disparate substantive behaviour and which involve different aetiologies. And central to realist criminology is that all parts of the square of crime must be linked up from the micro-level of interaction, to the mezzo-level (such as the nature of police bureaucracies or the informal economy in burgled goods) to the macro-level. From *The New Criminology* onwards we have consistently argued that criminology cannot remain on the micro-level, it must connect up with the wider domains, particularly the economic and the political.

This being said, many of the points of realism are applicable to other social science disciplines. The difficulty of social intervention is scarcely one which is limited to criminology. Indeed, the key problematic of realism is rooted in the shortcomings of social democratic attempts to engineer a more equitable social order.

References

Bhaskar, R. (1980) *A Realist Theory of Science*. Brighton: Harvester.

Blumstein, A. (1982) 'On the racial disproportionality of United States prison populations', *Journal of Criminal Law and Criminology*, 73: 1259–81.

Bonger, W. (1935) *An Introduction to Criminology*. London: Methuen.

Braithwaite, J. (1979) *Inequality, Crime and Public Policy*. London: Routledge & Kegan Paul.

Braithwaite, J. (1989) *Crime, Shame and Reintegration*. Cambridge: CUP.

Brown, D. and Hogg, R. (1992) 'Law and order politics', in R. Matthews and J. Young (eds), *Issues in Realist Criminology*. London: Sage.

Bunyan, T. (1976) *The Political Police in Britain*. London: Quartet.

Burney, E. (1990) *Putting Street Crime in its Place*. London: Centre for Inner City Studies, Goldsmiths' College, University of London.

Clarke, R. (1980) 'Statistical crime prevention: theory and practice', British Journal of Criminology, 20: 136–47.

Clinard, M. and Abbott, D. (1973) *Crime in Developing Countries*. New York: Wiley.

Cohen, A.K. (1965) 'The sociology of the deviant act', *American Sociological Review*, 30: 5–14.

Cohen, S. (1980) *Folk Devils and Moral Panics* (2nd edn). Oxford: Martin Robertson.

Cohen, S. (1990) *Intellectual Scepticism and Political Commitment*. Amsterdam: Universiteit.

Cohen, S. and Young, J. (1981) *The Manufacture of News* (rev. ed.). London: Routledge & Kegan Paul.

Corrigan, P., Jones, T., Lloyd, J. and Young, J. (1988) *Socialism, Merit and Efficiency*. London: Fabian Society.

Crawford, A., Jones, T., Woodhouse, T. and Young, J. (1990) *Second Islington Crime Survey*. Middlesex Polytechnic: Centre for Criminology.

Critical Criminologist (1990) Summer, 2(2).

Currie, E. (1985) *Confronting Crime*. New York: Pantheon Books.

Currie, E. (1990) 'Crime and market society'. Paper presented to the Conference on Crime and Policing, Islington, London.

Dorn, N. and South, N. (eds) (1987) *A Land fit for Heroin?* London: Macmillan.

Durkheim, E. (1952) *Suicide*. London: Routledge & Kegan Paul.

Eysenck, H. and Gudjonsson, G. (1989) *The Causes and Cures of Criminality*. New York: Plenum Press.

Felson, M. and Cohen, L. (1981) 'Modelling crime rates', *Research in Crime and Delinquency*, 18: 138–64.

Foucault, M. (1980) 'On popular justice', in C. Gordon (ed.) *Power/Knowledge*. Brighton: Harvester.

Genn, H. (1988) 'Multiple victimization' in M. Maguire and J. Pointing (eds) *Victims of Crime: a New Deal?* Milton Keynes: Open University Press.

Gilroy, P. and Sim, J. (1985) 'Law and order and the state of the left', *Capital and Class*, 25: 15–55.

Gouldner, A. (1971) *The Coming Crisis of Western Sociology*. London: Heinemann.

Government of Japan (1983) *Summary of the White Paper on Crime*. Tokyo: Research and Training Institute, Ministry of Justice.

Hacking, I. (1981) 'How should we do a history of statistics?', *Ideology and Consciousness*, 8: 15–26.

Hirschi, T. (1969) *Causes of Delinquency*. Berkeley: University of California Press.

Hough, M. (1986) 'Victims of violence and crime', in E. Fattah (ed.) *From Crime Policy to Victim Policy*. London: Macmillan.

Hough, M. and Mayhew, P. (1983) *The British Crime Survey*. London: HMSO.

Hulsman, L. (1986) 'Critical criminology and the concept of crime', *Contemporary Crises*, 10: 63–80.

Jones, T., Maclean, B. and Young, J. (1986) *The Islington Crime Survey*. Aldershot: Gower.

Kinsey, R., Lea, J. and Young, J. (1986) *Losing the Fight against Crime*. Oxford: Blackwell.

Lea, J. and Young, J. (1984) *What is to be Done about Law and Order?* Harmondsworth: Penguin.

Mathiesen, T. (1990) *The Politics of Abolition*. London: Martin Robertson.

Matthews. R. (1988) *Informal Justice?* London: Sage.

Matthews, R. (1989) 'Decarceration and penal reform', in P. Carlen and D. Cook (eds) *Paying for Crime*. Milton Keynes: Open University Press.

Matza, D. (1964) *Delinquency and Drift*. New York: Wiley.

Matza, D. (1969) *Becoming Deviant*. New Jersey: Prentice Hall.

Mills, C. Wright (1943) 'The professional ideology of social pathologists', *American Journal of Sociology*, 49(2).

Mooney, J. (1991) *Domestic Violence: Research Problems and Strategies*. Middlesex Polytechnic: Centre for Criminology.

Morris, P. and Heal, K. (1981) *Crime Control and the Police*. London: HMSO.

Painter, K. (1989) *Lighting and Crime: the Edmonton Project*. Middlesex Polytechnic: Centre for Criminology.

Painter, K., Lea, J., Woodhouse, T. and Young, J. (1989) *The Hammersmith Crime Survey*. Middlesex Polytechnic: Centre for Criminology.

Pearce, F. (1990) *Commercial and Conventional Crime in Islington*. Middlesex Polytechnic: Centre for Criminology.

Phipps, A. (1987) *Criminal Victimization, Crime Control and Political Action*. PhD thesis. Middlesex Polytechnic: Centre for Criminology.

Reiman, J. (1979) *The Rich get Rich and the Poor get Prison*. New York: Wiley.

Rosenbaum, D. (1986) *Community Crime Prevention*. London: Sage.

Sampson, A., Stubbs, P., Smith, D. and Pearson, G. (1985) 'Crime localities and multi-agency approach', *British Journal of Criminology*, 28: 478–93.

Schwartz, M. (1988) 'Aint't got no class: universal risk theories of battering', *Contemporary Crisis*, 12: 373–92.

Schwartz, M. (1990) 'US as compared to British Left Realism', *The Critical Criminologist*, 2: 5–12.

Scull, A. (1977) *Decarceration*. New Jersey: Prentice Hall.

Simon, W. and Gagnon, J. (1988) 'The anomie of affluence', *American Sociological Review*, 82: 356–78.

Smart, C. (1990) 'Feminist approaches to criminology', in L. Gelsthorpe and A. Morris (eds) *Feminist Perspectives in Criminology*. Milton Keynes: Open University Press.

Sparks, R. (1981) 'Surveys of victimization: an optimistic assessment', in M. Tonry and N. Morris (eds) *Crime and Justice Review*, Volume 3.

Sparks, R., Glenn, H. and Dodd, D. (1977) *Surveying Victims*. Chichester: Wiley.

Stevens, P. and Willis, C. (1979) *Race, Crime and Arrests*. London: HMSO.

Sumner, C. (1982) (ed.) *Crime, Justice and Underdevelopment*. Cambridge: Cambridge University Press.

Taylor, I. (1990) (ed.) *The Social Effects of Free Market Policies*. Hemel Hempstead: Harvester Wheatsheaf.

Taylor, I., Walton, P. and Young, J. (1973) *The New Criminology for a Social Theory of Deviance*. London: Routledge & Kegan Paul.

Thompson, E.P. (1980) *Writing by Candlelight*. London: Merlin.

Ward, D. and Kassebaum, G. (1966) *Women's Prison*. London: Weidenfeld and Nicolson.

Wheeler, S. (1967) 'Criminal statistics: a reformation of the problem', *Journal of Criminal Law, Criminology and Police Studies*, 58: 317–324.

Wilbanks, W. (1985) 'Is violent crime intraracial?' *Crime and Delinquency*, 31: 117–28.

Wilkins, L. (1964) *Social Deviance: Social Policy, Action and Research*. London: Tavistock.

Willis, P. (1977) *Learning to Labour*. Farnborough: Saxon House.

Wilson, J.Q. (1975) *Thinking About Crime*. New York: Vintage Books.

Wilson, J.Q. and Herrnstein, R. (1985) *Crime and Human Nature*. New York: Simon and Schuster.

Young, J. (1971) *The Drugtakers*. London: Paladin.

Young, J. (1974) 'New directions in subcultural theory', in J. Rex (ed.) *Approaches to Sociology*. London: Routledge & Kegan Paul.

Young, J. (1979) 'Left idealism, reformism and beyond', in B. Fine (ed.) *Capitalism and the Rule of Law*. London: Hutchinson.

Young, J. (1986) 'The failure of criminology: the need for radical realism', in R. Matthews and J. Young (eds) *Confronting Crime*. London: Sage.

Young, J. (1987) 'The tasks of a realist criminology', *Contemporary Crisis*, 11: 337–56.

Young, J. (1988a) 'Recent developments in criminology', In M. Haralambous (ed.) *Developments in Sociology*. Volume 4. Ormskirk: Causeway Press.

Young, J. (1988b) 'Risk of crime and fear of crime: the politics of victimization studies', in M. Maguire and J. Pointing (eds) *Victims of Crime: A New Deal*? Milton Keynes: Open University Press.

Young, J. (1988c) 'Radical criminology in Britain', in P. Rock (ed.) *The History of British Criminology*. Oxford: Clarendon Press.

Young, J. (1991) 'The rising demand for law and order and our Maginot lines of defence against crime', in N. Abercrombie and A. Warde (eds) *Social Change in Contemporary Britain*. Cambridge: Polity Press.

3 The analysis of crime

John Lea

Left realism in Britain originated as a call to socialists to 'take crime seriously' (Lea and Young, 1984; Young, 1986) under conditions in which criminality and other social problems facing the working class were worsening, while many radical criminologists remained obsessed with a social constructionist view of crime as simply a reflection of media-orchestrated moral panics or political diversion (Hall et al., 1976). However such an inspiration to take a problem seriously does not of itself constitute a new or an adequate theorization of the problem. The survival of left realism as a coherent criminology is dependent on its capacity to elaborate a body of theory which distinguishes it from other perspectives (see Figure 3.1).

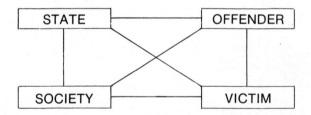

Figure 3.1

The development of theory in left realism in Britain in recent years has been largely concerned with the elaboration of a framework in which crime is analysed in terms of the interaction between four key variables: the state, social structure, offenders and victims. This framework has enabled left realism to establish a relationship with existing traditions of criminological theory by seeing much of the latter as partial perspectives focusing on particular elements of the interaction, rather than the process as a totality. Thus labelling theory tends to focus on the activities of the criminal justice system or society in labelling activities as criminal, classicism on the deterrent effects of the criminal justice system, much conservative theory on the efficacy of informal social control, positivism on the offender, and victimology on the characteristics of the victim. Each of these approaches may pose as a self-sufficient criminology, whereas each of them starts from an abstraction: one element of what is a more complex multi-faceted process (Young, 1987).

Such a framework is not presented as some theoretically neutral process of 'synthesis' of existing theory. The partiality of the latter is obviously only established from the standpoint of the more general interactionist framework of state, society, offender, victim. This framework itself is not immune from further elaboration and critique. It does not pose as a set of a priori categories defending themselves as the only logically possible coherent method for the study of crime. Rather it is a reflection of the existing division of labour in society and its legal system. The process of further theoretical development is not therefore simply a question of developing a more adequate set of categories but also of social change to which the criminologist both as theorist and policy maker is in no way external. The distinction for example between state and society is not an a priori one but a question of the structure of actually existing industrial societies. It is in no way external to the realist framework that the blurring and shifting of this distinction is a feature of modern societies, especially in the criminal justice area.

Defining the terms

It is necessary to give some preliminary definition of the concepts which form the framework of left realist analysis. By the 'state' is meant both the criminal justice agencies in the narrow sense and the state as political system in the more general sense. The latter is an important conduit for the reception from and transmission to other elements of the framework. In a similar way the term 'society' implies not only the micro-levels of family and community structure which may act as mechanisms of informal social control against crime but also the wider concept of 'civil society' as a set of legally, culturally and economically defined relations.

Offenders and victims are only at first sight simple concepts. The offender, it has to be remembered, is not necessarily an individual but may be a corporation, a political group or other organization. Likewise victims may be chosen as individuals or as members of groups defined in various ways. They may or may not be aware of their victimization or have accurate information concerning its source.

Action and reaction

What relations exist between the various components of the framework? Young (1987) identifies relations of 'action' and 'reaction' in which the state and the system of social control are structures which 'react' to the 'action' of offenders and victims, redefining their activities, devoting resources to their containment and so on and thereby playing an active role in the 'production' of the final level of crime in society. This relationship is an attempt to transcend the conflict between, on the one hand, varieties of labelling theory which see changes in crime rates as a result of some combination of the activities of criminal justice agencies and social perceptions and, on the other, a positivism which speaks only of 'real' changes in the numbers of offenders and victims.

This approach can be made more concrete by seeing both sides as engaging in action and reaction. Society and the state do not simply respond to the problem of crime but also engage in various pre-emptive activities in the causation and definition of crime. Likewise the behaviour of both offenders and victims can be seen as not only constituting 'problematic situations' to which the state and the system of social control may react but also themselves responding and reacting to the state and the system of social control. It is of course the case that society and the state are determinant 'in the last instance', in the sense that victims and offenders do not exist except as recognized by some combination of legal and social definition whereas the state and social structure are not derived from the existence of offenders and victims.[1]

The state and society

The existence of crime: the process of criminalization
The creation of the categories of criminality is obviously the most fundamental action of both the state and society. The criminal law can be seen as a language describing certain types of social actions and providing legitimation for the existence and activity of state agencies in their relations with individuals as offenders, victims, witnesses, holders of relevant information, etc. In addition to the content of the law the rules of procedure for the establishment of culpability themselves help determine the parameters within which social problems can be dealt with through a strategy of criminalization. The fact that criminal justice systems largely deal with relations between individual agents rather than social groups per se, the rules of presentation of evidence, proof in criminal trials as well as those governing the conduct of the trial (such as rules of cross-examination), all serve to determine what types of problems can be effectively dealt with by the criminal justice system.

Within a given legal code and its rules of procedure the agencies of law enforcement and justice enjoy a considerable leeway of discretion. They do not simply respond to crime but, in making decisions about what types of crime to respond to and by what means, they act as a positive determinant of the pattern of criminality. There is thus a de facto criminalization of activities by state agencies, which is of equal importance to the formal legal status of actions as crimes. The degree of correspondence of the two depends on the constitutional and actual accountability of the agencies, the forms of operational discretion available to them, such as the autonomy of judges and prosecutors, the operational independence of police chiefs, the day-to-day relationship between criminal justice agencies and various social groups, and the structure of criminal activities themselves. There is what might be called 'over-criminalization' associated with the development of particular operational policing strategies, in which whole communities are treated as if they were offenders, through for example the use of random 'stop and search' techniques (Lea and Young, 1984). Likewise criminal courts may tend to pre-judge the guilt of offenders from particular social groups. A reverse process might be called 'under-criminalization' whereby some types of crime (such as domestic violence, neighbour disputes) are defined by police as 'rubbish crime' and not really worth dealing with, certain areas of the city may go relatively unpoliced, or offences by powerful corporations may go unprosecuted.

Alongside the state agencies and the language of criminal law, society also has its language which defines particular behaviours as crime. The extent to which the language of ordinary social interaction overlaps with that of the criminal law is complex. Some abolitionists (Hulsman, 1986) like to imagine that the criminal law is quite redundant and that society has its own language of 'problematic situations' which is autonomous from and superior to that of the criminal law. It does not seem likely that the language of interpersonal disputes can replace that of the criminal law when ordinary citizens may not be able to agree on spontaneous definitions of situations (such as when does physical violence constitute assault?) or be otherwise confused as to the nature and extent of their victimization.

In democratic societies the criminal law might be expected simply to reproduce and echo social sanctions. But where society is divided by structures of class and power the criminal law can be both a progressive and a reactionary force. It may import the language of criminality into some areas where ordinary language, reflecting established power relations of class or gender, is blind to the existence of conflict and harm while in other areas it may turn a blind eye to situations criminalized by ordinary discourse.

Indeed rapid social change may produce conditions in which the same activity is both criminalized and to some extent still sanctioned by social values. For example, the morality associated with traditional family structures may still tolerate a certain amount of violence by husbands against wives even when the advance of democratic rights and the political influence of feminist movements combine to sensitize society to the rights of married women as citizens to defence against violence from their husbands. These conflicts are reflected in the working of the criminal justice system with the result that a formal acknowledgement of a problem is often combined with a practical reluctance of agencies to act effectively despite a formal requirement to do so.

Reaction: the response to changing social problems The process of creation of the categories of criminality by the interaction of state and society involves, in modern industrial societies, a process of constant reaction and adaptation to social changes. While there may be considerable stability in general ideas of crime or harm, there are substantial changes in how, and to which activities, such categories are to be applied. Social and political movements may result in simultaneous pressure on the state to expel the concepts of criminality from some areas (such as soft drugs) and bring it more strongly into others (such as marital rape) or, on the level of the day-to-day activities of criminal justice agencies, devote more resources to the containment of some crimes and less to others. Such dynamics, unfortunately for abolitionists, do not seem to result in any general reduction in the role of the criminal justice system vis-à-vis the containment of social problems.

The existence of offenders and victims
Having established the categories of criminal behaviour both the state and society respond and attempt to contain criminal activity itself. But at the same time the creation of such activity, for all but the most hardened biological positivist, is a product of society. The fact is that modern industrial societies put as much effort, albeit unconsciously, into the creation of crime as they do to its containment.

Action: the production of potential offenders and victims
There are a number of respects in which criminal activity has to be seen as a product of the normal working of state and social processes rather than their 'breakdown'. Even the commission of crimes by the criminal justice system itself should not be thought of as solely a characteristic of authoritarian states or 'states of emergency' in which normal legality is suspended. Violation of criminal law by state security

agencies, albeit concealed, appears to be a normal enough activity even in liberal democratic states (Wright, 1987; Chambliss, 1989).

More important for the study of 'ordinary' crime, however, are the unintended consequences of the normal functioning of criminal justice institutions, of which the most obvious example is that of the prison as the producer of crime through its latent function as a channel for the socialization of the inmate into established criminal subcultures. Other examples are to be found in the unintended consequences of the activities of law enforcement agencies. Young described the 'deviancy amplification' effect whereby tough policing strategies against soft drug users drove the latter further into criminal activity (Young, 1971). More generally, one of the effects of the 'over-criminalization' mentioned above may be that of legitimizing offences which are seen by local communities as resistance to heavy and indiscriminate policing.

However it is predominantly at the level of social structure rather than state institutions that the major causes of criminal activity are to be found. It is important to note that left realism has not hitherto attempted to elaborate any new theory of the causes of crime; rather the strategy has been that of elaborating and adapting existing bodies of theory into the 'action and reaction' model. A major influence has been the theory of anomie or relative deprivation derived from the classic contributions of Merton (1938) and Cloward and Ohlin (1960), combined with a theory of social and economic marginality. Relative deprivation, a conflict between socially diffused goals and needs and the restricted availability of the legitimate means for their achievement would probably be resolved by a turn to criminality among those groups additionally marginalized from participation in the political processes of modern industrial societies (Lea and Young, 1984).

Serious critics of left realist criminology have pointed to the restricted applicability of the theory to particular areas of crime. Street crime such as household burglary, shoplifting, and street robbery are those which come most readily to mind when considering relative deprivation as 'illegal means to socially sanctioned goals'. However, relative deprivation theory as developed by Cloward and Ohlin (1960) and others saw the causes of delinquency not so much in an instrumental response to deprivation as might be evidenced by engaging in burglary as an income supplement, but in the development of a subculture in which alternative values develop precisely as a way of coping with the frustrations of exclusion from legitimate routes to success. In this sense the role of interpersonal 'expressive' violence, or ritualized forms of conspicuous consumption as ways of establishing status in the absence of conventional means and symbols can be understood. Also 'crimes of passion' such as homicide, and interpersonal violence such as sexual assault and rape, have a concentration among the poor and deprived and can be seen as arising from dynamics of relative deprivation. Box describes the dynamics of rape by men from poor and deprived backgrounds:

> When men from this latter group rape they rely primarily on physical violence because this is the resource they command. Being relatively unable to 'wine and dine' females or place them in a position of social debt, and being less able to induce in women a sense of physical and emotional over-comeness these 'socially' powerless men are left with a sense of resentment and bitterness which is fanned and inflamed by cultural sex-role stereotypes of 'successful' men being sexually potent. (Box, 1983: 152)[2]

However there are important areas of criminality to which theories of relative deprivation and marginality might be thought inapplicable. 'What does anomie contribute to the analysis of organized crime or of so-called white collar crime?' asks Tamar Pitch (1987). In fact quite a lot, at least as regards organized crime, though it is true that left realists have yet to do substantial work in this area. It is worth remembering that, as Arlacchi (1987) has recently noted, one of the impulses to the work of relative deprivaton theory, especially at the time Merton was developing his account in the USA, was the attempt to combat the widespread 'alien culture' view of organized criminality as associated with Italian immigrants rather than the internal dynamics of US society. Relative deprivation theory presupposed socialization into the values of mainstream US culture. The adaptation of relative depri-vation theory by Lea and Young (1984) was for a very similar purpose: that of rebutting the media image of the 'alien culture' of young blacks as a cause of street crime in British cities.

However it is true that a too-close association between relative deprivation and socio-political marginality leads to a restricted focus on disorganized street crime. Organized crime may originate in and recruit from social groups marginalized from legitimate opportunity structures, but once established is able to secure a measure of stability in its environment through protection, bribery, or threats of violence, and a degree of penetration of legitimate financial and political institutions (Catanzaro, 1988; Santino, 1989). To deploy the term 'marginality' at this stage is purely rhetorical and means little more than that the activity is illegal.[3] Indeed successful organized crime as a structure of illegal opportunities for the accumulation of wealth and status is better understood in this context as a form of demarginali-zation.

This analysis seems to be in accordance with Cloward and Ohlin's classic treatment in which a distinction between the criminal career and the criminality of the disorganized – or marginalized – slum is stressed. 'Among the environmental supports of a criminal style of life are integration of offenders at various age levels and close integration of the carriers of conventional and illegitimate values', while 'Just as the un-integrated slum cannot mobilize legitimate resources for the young neither can it provide them with access to stable criminal careers for illegitimate learning and opportunity structures do not develop' (Cloward and Ohlin, 1960: 162, 173).

White-collar and business crime paradoxically present less problem for the theory of anomie and relative deprivation than does street crime. As far as the latter is concerned one of the main criticisms of the Mertonian approach was that of the plurality of values in the cultures of modern industrial societies and the consequent implausibility of attributing criminality to innovatory attempts to achieve the goal of economic success (Lemert, 1967). This criticism has suffered from declining plausibility with the expansion of mass media and education disseminating standardized expectations. But, as Box remarked, the modern capitalist corporation never suffered from the problem of ambiguity concerning its goal of profit maximization: 'This defining characteristic – it is a goal seeking entity – makes a corporation inherently criminogenic for it necessarily operates in an uncertain and unpredictable environment such that its purely legitimate opportunities for goal attainment are sometimes limited and constrained' (Box, 1983: 35; Passas, 1990). At this level marginality becomes, in Stan Cohen's phrase, a 'mickey mouse concept' (Cohen, 1985). Worse, it can fulfil an ideological function in denying the criminogenic nature of the capitalist system itself by implying that crime is always only a product of breakdown or absence of 'normal' social or political structures, whereas in fact for powerful corporations violation of the criminal law or pressure on governments to legalize activities technically 'criminal' are strategies often pursued in combination (Pearce, 1976).

The context of white-collar and corporate crime emphasizes that relative deprivation is not to be confused with material poverty. The frustration of inability to meet expected goals and norms of 'success' is diffused throughout all social classes in a capitalist society. The young middle-class business executive who takes out his failings in the competitive arena by violence towards his wife or children, or in bouts of public drinking, is no less a victim of relative deprivation than the inner-city mugger. The emphasis here is on 'relative'.

However, this brings us to the second weak spot identified by critics: the question of the precise mechanisms whereby high levels of relative deprivation and, in a subset of cases, marginality are linked to the commission of criminal acts (Pitch, 1987; de Leo, 1987). An account of the production of potential offenders has to be supplemented by an account of the production of criminal opportunities. The theory of relative deprivation, precisely because of the wide range of its application, cannot explain the particular types of crime that occurs unless supplemented by a theory of criminal opportunities into which those suffering from such deprivation may move.

The study of crime as a structure of opportunities has been one of the preoccupations of rational choice theory. While some criminologists – economists in particular – have attempted to portray rational choice theory as a self-sufficient general account of criminal behaviour, such an approach usually find it necessary to make a prior distinction between those who would or would not take advantage of – or seek out – criminal opportunities. Thus Becker's classic analysis of rational choice theory applied to criminology (Becker, 1968), having claimed that '... a useful theory of criminal behaviour can dispense with special theories of anomie ... and simply extend the economist's usual analysis of choice', proceeded to add 'willingness to commit an illegal act' as a variable in the formula for the calculus of rationality of criminal action. The best approach seems therefore to regard accounts of the production of potential offenders and accounts of the production of criminal opportunities as essentially complementary and interdependent aspects of the process whereby society produces crime.

Two key components of the criminal opportunity structure can be distinguished. First, the existence of a demand on the part of both criminals and the non-criminal public for illegal commodities or services (drugs, vice, arms, etc), or for legal commodities illegally acquired: that is, the existence of the criminal economy. Secondly, a source of legitimate – from the standpoint of offenders – victims who are 'fair game' as targets for crime or situations in which criminal violence is seen as justified. In this respect it is a mistake to see the 'criminal subculture' or the 'subculture of violence' as entirely isolated from dominant values. The dominant culture provides a set of labels which, though not directly legitimizing crime, enables the offender to elaborate his or her own legitimation. Thus the murder of a prostitute is considered less socially obnoxious than that of a 'respectable' woman.[4] Social groups defined as 'outsiders' may become particular targets for crime (as in racial attacks). At the level of corporate crime particular state agencies such as tax authorities or other national states, particularly in the Third World, may be seen as legitimate victims for corruption, low safety standards, dumping of hazardous products, etc (Braithwaite, 1984; Jones, 1988).

There is often a close relationship between the legitimacy of victims and their vulnerability. The former may be a cause of the latter as where racial prejudice legitimizes violence against ethnic minorities, maximizes vulnerability by assuring them that the victim is likely to get little support – for instance from neighbours in cases of racial harassment on housing estates – and at the same time relegates ethnic minorities to the most criminogenic areas of the city. The two may run parallel as where the weak law enforcement capacities of some Third World states parallels their legitimacy as victims in the eye of multi-national corporations. The two may also conflict as with elderly people in large cities living lonely isolated lives with a high vulnerability to crimes such as burglary and mugging, or young women having to walk home during unsocial hours with a high vulnerability to rape – though in both cases such crimes are regarded as particularly vicious by society at large.

A final important component of legitimation of victims concerns the attribution of responsibility for the criminal act itself. Victim blaming and 'victim precipitation' can be regarded as the polar case of the legitimate victim in which the latter rather than the offender comes to be regarded as the cause of the crime. Such an ideological construct needs to be carefully distinguished from the fact that many offences may arise out of prior interaction in which both victim and offender participate.

Reaction: deterrence, control and support for victims

Both the state and society react to crime, attempting to control and contain that which they have produced. An orthodox distinction would see the state as the sphere of law and legitimate force aimed largely at detection and deterrence with society as the sphere of informal social control and prevention. This distinction is in fact blurred in a number of ways. The operation of state agencies even at the most 'technical' level rests on assumptions concerning social relations. The state itself may attempt to initiate, and organize, informal crime prevention measures by citizens ranging from sur-veillance, dispute resolution, to 'community courts' (Matthews, 1988). The motives of particular governments in taking such initiatives may include those of attempting solutions to what are considered growing legitimation or fiscal problems faced by criminal justice agencies. Finally the boundaries between state and private institutions become increasingly blurred through the development of intermediate struc-tures of surveillance and control (Cohen, 1985).

The deterrent effect of the criminal law cannot be considered independent of its relationship to collective moral sentiment. Where the criminal code reflects moral sentiments widespread in society then the simple fact of illegality itself has a deterrent effect, although this may be mediated by factors such as the general social status of the offender and the absence of feelings of guilt or shame (Braithwaite, 1989) with a consequent reluctance on the part of the criminal justice system to act forcefully in such areas (Johnson, 1986). Although the severity of the penalty may have some deterrent effect, attempts in research to specify this have been inconclusive (Cook, 1980). What is reasonably established however is that it is less the penalties for particular offences prescribed by the law than the certainty of detection which constitutes the bulk of the deterrent effect. The certainty of detection itself has both technical and social components. The social component concerns the general willingness of individuals to give information and report crime to the police, appear as witnesses in court, etc. This depends on the relations between police and local communities, on the relations of power between victims and offenders and on the socioeconomic structure of localities determining such matters as the daily movement of population and the likelihood of crimes being witnessed (Cohen and Felson, 1979).

An important social and political component of crime detection concerns the nature of the terrain on which they are committed. The political power and surveillance capacities of a state are not necessarily evenly spread throughout its terrain. In Third World countries the de facto power of the criminal justice system may be concentrated in urban centres. In the large cities of modern industrial societies, economic changes over the last 50 years have produced an 'internal periphery' in the older urban areas in which high unemployment, political and social marginalization, alienation from criminal justice and welfare state agencies, high rates of crime and other social problems are concentrated. Police operations in both types of areas may frequently take the form of episodic military expedition rather than regular patrolling.

Analogous problems arise when the terrain over which the crime takes place exceeds the geographical boundaries of the state. Modern computer-assisted financial crime usually involves sophisticated movement of funds on a world scale, and tracing the activities of criminals (as in the case of the 'laundering' of profits from drug traffic) may involve cooperation between the criminal justice systems of several nation states. The differences between states both in terms of the content of law and in the efficiency of criminal justice agencies may enable certain types of offenders to select the terrain on which they operate or focus the illegal aspects of their international activities (Braithwaite, 1984).

The technical questions that concern detection are numerous. Money is difficult to trace, especially if it is nothing other than electronically stored information. Unique antique art objects are more easily traceable. Between these polar cases stands the vast bulk of 'mass private property' of motor vehicles, televisions, etc, which in their identity may present problems of traceability akin to that of money. Secondly there is the process whereby the crime is committed. In modern business fraud the specialist skills required to detect and assemble the evidence of the crime are considerable and pose a problem for police forces considered as generic multi-task bureaucracies. A different type of complexity can be seen in crimes committed within the family, such as child sexual abuse, where the evidence may be ambiguous and depend on medical judgement. In both areas policing has become increasingly 'multi-agency', involving experts and agencies from outside the criminal justice system.

A crucial question both for criminological theory and policy making is the extent to which the average 'solvability' of crime is decreasing. Technical questions of solvability may in fact be social factors in disguise. How much of the alleged – by police – decrease in solvability of household burglary (Newman, 1983) is due to the untraceability of mass private property and how much to the fact that the state of police–community relations reduces the flow of information from public to police is difficult to assess. Nevertheless, the hypothesis of an increase in the amount of crime coupled with a general decline in solvability would certainly account for the recent popularity of the preventive approach to crime control. Other 'technical' problems are ultimately questions of social relations. The complexity of computer bank frauds is in the last instance a question of the secrecy and discretion dictated by the regime of competition in industrial and financial capitalism. The problem of detecting stolen 'mass commodities' such as TV sets or video recorders is a question of the development of an economy of illegal consumer goods into which such items, once inserted, become just commodities like any other, and the 'technical' problem of diagnosing child sexual abuse is at root one of the relations of power and collusion in family relations.

Like crime detection, prevention has both social and technical dimensions. What all preventive strategies have in common is the attempt to prevent the activity of criminal offenders by means of measures which apply to all individuals irrespective of intention. Traditionally, prevention strategies have been conceived of as technically based and concerned with target hardening, which consists in the identification of potential targets (usually buildings, vehicles, safes, computer programs, etc), and making them generally difficult to penetrate without the cooperation of the appropriate authority. Time locks, entry phones, computer passwords, are all of this nature. A large part of the skills of the professional criminal are concerned with the ability to circumnavigate such obstacles. Screening focuses on the people entering or leaving a particular area, or area of activity, which is vulnerable to crime. Employees leaving a workplace may be subject to random searches as a measure against pilferage, passengers entering commercial aircraft will have their baggage searched as an anti-terrorist measure. Many technical target-hardening devices provide an automatic opportunity for screening: the owner of an answer-phone system can refuse entry to those who arouse suspicion. Again, the skills of the criminal are largely dedicated to outwitting such measures. Burglars may penetrate answer-phone systems by posing as public officials. Terrorist bombs made out of non-detectable explosive carefully disguised as cassette recorders may penetrate baggage control systems. General surveillance and visibility may be increased by the use of video cameras, as in shopping precincts, railway stations, etc, by improving street lighting to increase visibility, by architectural changes to remove some of the spatial opportunities for crime mentioned above, or by attempts to mobilize residents in a local neighbourhood into neighbourhood watch schemes to keep an eye open for suspicious circumstances and increase the flow of information to the police.

The operation of technical crime prevention measures always has a crucial social element. The numbers of people and the nature of their use of public space determines the way in which geographical and architectural factors may act as a deterrent to crime (Jacobs, 1962; Newman, 1972; Coleman, 1986). A newly installed system of entry phones and door locks may, by impeding movement, increase the isolation of elderly people, and so escalate their fear of and their vulnerability to crime. A sophisticated factory or airport security system may easily be undermined if the quality or working conditions of the labour force does not match the sophistication of the equipment. Neighbourhood watch schemes designed to increase surveillance will fail if the majority of people are absent from the area during the times when crimes are most likely to be committed (Cohen and Felson, 1979), or simply do not look out of their windows. Increasing the intensity of street lighting enables rapists and muggers to see their victims more clearly every bit as much as it enables ordinary citizens to see where they are going. A purely 'technicist' attitude to crime prevention is incapable of understanding why the same technical innovation works on some occasions and not others, because it fails to grasp how technical 'effects' are always mediated through the social relations between people (Lea, 1986).

Social crime prevention, so-called, is a more recent innovation. Its basic aim is to construct or reconstruct as a deliberate aim of social policy the type of social relations, usually at a micro-level within a neighbourhood of a city, that are thought to maximize social pressure against crime. Neighbourhood watch schemes are seen to have a social cohesion effect as much as an opportunity reduction effect by increasing the occasions for neighbourly cooperation in the production of newsletters and other means of disseminating information. Such informal bonding increases peoples' confidence in their locality, and they are more likely to be out on the streets taking an interest in what is going on, and hence increase the informal controls against crime. Even the state agencies such as the police by their very presence (irrespective of their crime detection activities) can be seen to contribute to a sense of public security and so help create a self-reinforcing process of greater public security and diminishing crime (Wilson, 1983). Some governments have attempted to infuse an element of legal coercion in the creation of such informal control. Obviously the 'neighbourhood' or 'community' cannot be an object (yet) of legal regulation, but the family can. Proposals to increase the responsibility of parents for the conduct of their children will, it is thought, give some legal backing to the 'reconstruction' of informal social control. A final dimension of social prevention is the tendency in recent years to identify a crime prevention aspect of almost any activity that occupies people harmlessly, as with youth clubs, summer camps, etc.

At the other end of the criminal spectrum preventive strategies have been deployed as strategies against corporate crime. The granting of licensing powers to business, trade or financial investment associations with the associated activities of surveillance and monitoring is regarded as an effective, if not preferred, method of crime control to that of criminal investigation (Clarke, 1983; Levi, 1987). It is here that we should expect to find some of the problems of strategies of social prevention clearly illustrated. In the sphere of corporate crime those entrusted with the role of prevention are not clearly differentiated from those likely to engage in criminal activities. The question is not so much that of positive collusion as the failure of a normative system of control to impede criminality because it implicitly sanctions it (Pearce, 1976). This is illustrated in the duplicity of the corporate criminal offender's role where in the broader social structure he also appears as an exemplar of the good law-abiding citizen (Solivetti, 1987).

In the prevention of street crime analogous problems prevail. Neighbourhood watch schemes are biased in the direction of household burglary and vehicle theft, with an inbuilt tendency to view the offender as an outsider to the neighbourhood (LRET, 1986; Rosenbaum, 1987). Such schemes ignore crimes such as domestic violence because the latter are shielded by conventions of non-interference in the private sphere. Crime prevention discourse also frequently reinforces the separation, increasingly arbitrary, between street crime and organized crime, by imagining a world consisting only of the former. Against organized drug-dealing networks neighbourhood watch may be rather ineffective.

In other negative ways crime prevention strategies may reproduce the patterns of social inequality and victimization which they seek to combat. Those areas with the highest rates of street crime are the hardest areas in which to establish preventive initiatives precisely because such areas also suffer heavily from other social problems like unemployment, poverty, poor housing, etc. Physical crime prevention may therefore fall victim to general decay of housing stock and streets while the lack of a sense of community, the prevalence of ethnic conflict and so on may either impede participation or make it highly unrepresentative. The long-run effect may be simply the displacement of crime into the poorest and most socially disorganized areas of cities where crime prevention is ineffective. Meanwhile, in the area of corporate crime regulatory bodies may end up simply displacing crime (that is, dumping unsafe products, violation of safety standards, etc) to those areas of the Third World where all such 'surveillance' is powerless to act.

The state reacts not only to offenders but also to victims. It reacts most effectively to those considered as illegitimate victims, though in this respect state agencies may not necessarily duplicate definitions of the victim nor prioritize the forms of victimization widespread in society. This may be both due to the particular class and group interests or cultural values that predominate in the state and to forms of rationality which determine the distribution of resources. Where the state does not recognize those forms of victimization defined as such by significant social groups then alternative forms of victim support are likely to develop – battered women's refuges, rape crisis centres, among others. These may then in turn become the basis for the organization of social movements around victimization to change the priorities of state activity.

Offenders and victims

It is one-dimensional to see crime and victimization as simply the product, or end result, of a particular set of social or other determinants. A great deal of criminology has been preoccupied with the aetiology of crime. This is only one side of the square of crime. The sociology of crime cannot rest at the sociology of the production of crime but must recognize the relative autonomy of crime, both as a subcultural phenomenon and as a form of economy with its own dynamics of reproduction and change, and the capacity to affect not only its immediate victims but society and the state in general. Just as the state and society can react and respond to crime, so can crime react and respond to the state and society.

Relations between offenders and their victims

Entirely random victimization is rare: the crazed gunman who walks down a street shooting at random is not the typical criminal offender. Most offenders have some social or economic relationship to their victims. They may live with them as in domestic violence or spousal murder, they may live in the same neighbourhood as with most opportunist street crime or street violence, they may identify them as an economically suitable target in terms of the aims of criminal enterprise as with bank robbery or commercial fraud, or they may be in some economic market relationship such as that of customer or competitor. An understanding of the relations between victims and offenders is crucial to explaining both the perceived impact of crime and many of the problems associated with its detection. A useful way of classifying such relations is in terms of whether the offender is an individual or an institution and whether the victimization takes place as a result of direct intention or is indirect; that is to say it occurs as the unintended result of the pursuit of other goals. The most obvious case of victimization where the offender is an individual and the victimization direct is murder or physical assault. Indeed 'crime' as such is frequently thought of as predominantly actions of this type. Domestic burglary involves a less direct relationship between victim and offender – they may not meet, but the offender is an individual, the offence is intended and the target is subject to a degree of selection.

By contrast much so-called corporate crime involving the offender as an organization involves indirect victimization.[5] The ignoring of safety regulations is undertaken from the normal corporate goal of profit maximization, and the assumption is generally that the organization can function successfully without them. That is not to say that corporate decision makers are unaware of the likely victimization consequences of their actions. They may quite cynically calculate that 'if' people die as a result of corporate actions few consequences will fall on the corporation because of the dependence of the government, for example in a Third World country, on the presence of that corporation. Alternatively a calculation may simply be made of the chances of 'accidents' occurring and risks taken. Here corporate crime begins to move towards direct victimization where a company quite deliberately markets a product it knows to be unsafe, as with the notorious Ford Pinto case (Cullen et al., 1987), or engages in the bribery of governments, assassination of trade union organizers, etc. Individual victimization can of course be indirect, as in drunken driving manslaughter or other forms of victimization resulting from individual failure to anticipate the consequences of actions.

Victims, like offenders, may be individuals or groups. The individual victim of rape or murder stands out in the community and whether he or she is shunned or supported by the immediate community depends on many factors noted already. The victim may be seen as chosen only because of membership of a group – as in racial harassment. This is likely to maximize community support. In other cases where a group is being victimized, for example the consumers of contaminated products, the spread of victimization may be a factor in hiding, at least for a period, some of its impact since individuals are unaware of differences in their own situations compared to those of other similar people.

Action: the impact of crime
The impact of crime is perceived not as some simple observable body of facts but through the interaction between society, the state and victims themselves. State agencies seek objective measurable criteria such as average likelihood of victimization, average value to property lost in burglary or criminal damage, etc. The question of resource distribution between alternative areas of social policy creates a pressure towards a form of measurement in terms of which the impact of a vast array of social problems can be compared. Translation of the impact of crime into monetary terms enables governments to make comparable estimates of the 'seriousness' of different crime problems, and of crime generally in relation to other problems competing for public resources. However there are good and bad ways of making such calculations. Statistical averages over a whole country can be misleading because different types of crime are unevenly distributed and have different types of impact. Such calculations as 'the average citizen stands a chance of being a victim of crime once every 400 years' and 'the average property lost by burglary and theft is £50' can become part of a political strategy which minimizes the impact of crime and society, ignores that it is the poor and marginalized who are the major victims of crime and is unaware that the same value of property stolen from a poor person obviously has a greater impact than if stolen from a wealthy person (Kinsey et al., 1986).

However, the opposite strategy of allowing the victims to define impact of crime through simple responses to social survey questions has drawbacks and may in fact embody a similar relationship between victim and state – one of marginality and lack of political power – as that embodied in statistical averages of property values lost in burglary. Social surveys assume that victims are conscious of their victimization. In terms of the classification of victim–offender relations outlined above it is obviously the direct and individual forms of offending that victims will be most aware of. This can result in ignoring many forms of corporate crime of which victims may be unaware in the short run, or which may simply appear as 'accidents' to anyone not familiar with legal regulations or the processes of corporate decision making, and where the extent of victimization – as for example with illegal environmental pollution – may only become clear over a number of years.

The impact of crime on victims is closely allied to the question of the fear of crime. State researchers making statistical calculations of 'risk rates' in the manner noted above often come to the conclusion that citizens have an 'exaggerated' fear of crime in terms of their 'real exposure'. Quite apart from the problems already mentioned of using statistical averages a crucial issue concerns how far the victim is seen as idiosyncratic or as a typical member of a social group. Where the victim is regarded as 'legitimate' – in the sense previously discussed – or as having provoked the offence him or herself, then the impact of the crime on others in terms of increasing the fear that similar victimization will occur to them will also be minimized. Fear will be maximized not only where the victim is seen as representative or typical but where the offence is seen as linked to other offences. Women as a group are more frightened of burglary than men, not because they are more irrational at calculating risk rates than men but because for a woman, encountering a burglar may involve also the risk of rape or sexual assault, whereas more men may feel they could scare off the offender. Women thus tend to have more similar rates of fear across the spectrum of different types of crime than do men (Warr, 1985), and they are quite rational so to do. This is not to say that fear of crime, or lack of it, is always rational. Where the impact of crime is not immediately grasped as such it will not be feared. The irrationality of victims' fear is more likely to err on the side of underestimating crime by ignoring the impact of corporate crime than it is to exaggerate the importance of street crime.

Fear of crime has its own impact, the most important of which is a de facto curfew on movements around the city, especially after dark, coupled with feelings of insecurity even within the home. The unintended consequences of fewer people on the streets may well be to contribute further to the social decay of the area and to increase the likelihood of street crime (Wilson, 1983).

Neither the impact of crime nor the rationality of fear can be adequately measured by the most frequently used techniques of average risk rates or victim surveys. Both may underestimate the real importance of crime in people's lives unless they are seen as one, albeit important, input to the democratic process where such exists, that is most capable of enabling ordinary people and their elected representatives to become aware of the extent of crime and its real impact on society. In all societies in which, even with the formal trappings of democracy, the media of communication are monopolized and distorted and even fear of crime becomes itself a means to other political ends, this will not be achieved.

Reaction: victim mobilization

A cardinal principle of social stability in modern industrial societies embodied in the criminal law is that it is the state rather than the victim that responds to crime. The victim in most criminal legal codes exists as witness for the state. Crime prevention strategies can be pursued by anyone because they are aimed at citizens in general as long as they are not of a punitive nature and do not infringe civil liberties, such as the right of way in public spaces. However the legitimacy of state agencies may be compromised in particular sections of society due to their partisanship or inefficiency, and may give rise in extreme cases to the growth of vigilante or other forms of self-policing with the support of victims and those who fear victimization. In revolutionary situations such organs may approach the status of embryonic alternative criminal justice systems (Santos, 1980) directly challenging the existing state. Under less dramatic conditions such alternatives may become easily coopted or out-manoeuvred by the adaptations from existing criminal justice agencies. In a similar way social groups perceiving that the state does not take their victimization seriously enough may develop forms of alternative victim support as illustrated by the growth of rape crisis centres and voluntary refuges for women victims of domestic violence. These may in turn become the basis for political campaigns around victimization and may in the long run accept funding from or be incorporated into a quasi-official relationship with the state.

Offenders, victims, society and the state

Alongside the impact of crime on its victims is its impact on society and the state. These two are frequently not distinguished, victims after all are members of society, the fear of crime and its consequences extends beyond those immediately victimized, and the criminal justice system and various state-financed victim support services divert social resources to deal with the consequences of crime. However, as noted above, it is important sociologically to understand criminality as a form of social behaviour, as a subsystem of society, in fact as a 'normal' part of social activity which acts to reproduce itself and defend the conditions of its own existence. It is otherwise difficult to understand the continuity of various types of criminality in modern societies.

Action: reproducing the social structure of offenders and victims

Crimes of passion do not generally exist as a particular form of social activity with their own economy, subculture and division of labour. Spousal murder or domestic violence might be thought of as arising spontaneously out of the dynamics of the individuals involved in destructive marital relationships. This simply means that the social structure and culture which sustains such criminal activity, namely the modern family and its associated patriarchal values and stresses and strains on personal relations, is generally diffused throughout the social system, a point that feminists have frequently emphasized. A similar point could be made about much commercial crime which is produced by the entirely normal values of business organization and methods.

At the other end of the spectrum are the elaborate organizations of international organized crime and its leading edge: the illegal drugs and armaments trade. While not part of normal – or legal – capitalist enterprise, it is precisely the similarity of the manufacture and trade in dangerous and illegal commodities to legitimate enterprise in terms of the extended chain of production, marketing and financing which requires measures to be taken to secure the continuity and predictability of such enterprise in the face of determined – although hitherto unsuccessful – attempts by law enforcement agencies to interdict. In the centre of this continuum are various types of criminal semi-economies with varying degrees of organization, such as localized trade in stolen consumer goods like video-recorders or credit cards. The more organized and continuous over time the criminal activity the more 'security-conscious' it is forced to become, and the more steps it must take to secure its conditions of existence. Within these criminal economies all the usual dynamics of competition and amalgamation pertain. Such criminal economies, in order to secure their continuity, have to both secure the compliance of local populations and neutralize the criminal justice system.

Securing the compliance of local populations depends in the first instance on the nature of the criminal activity. If it is one that members of the local community can benefit from compliance may not even be a problem: few people in any locality are going to complain at the presence of cheap tape cassettes or video-recorders for sale. If the activity is one that the local population is in principle opposed to then other steps will have to be taken. The narco-capitalists of Medellin and other Latin American drug production centres invest a considerable number of dollars in local schools, social and health care centres, and other forms of 'Robin Hood' activities which, combined with violence and terror, aim at the maintenance of a quiescent local population. In the older traditional Mafia regions of Sicily and Calabria mafiosi traditionally maintained their status in the community as 'men of honour' by helping local citizens sort out legitimate grievances with the authorities or with powerful landowners (Arlacchi, 1988; Hess, 1973). In a similar way powerful criminal organizations may finance political parties or particular candidates sympathetic to their interests, both at a national and regional level.

Alongside the activities of powerful criminal organizations the criminal economy may exercise its own form of social control by bringing employment and income to marginalized groups who would otherwise be unemployed. Mike Davis's graphic description of a large city in the United States in which, as the dynamics of the modern capitalist economy moved legitimate employment out of the older urban areas, young male black teenagers have become the main family breadwinners through being able to avail themselves of the only form of well-paid economic activity in the area – street dealing in cocaine and its derivatives (Davis, 1988).

Reaction: containing and galvanizing the state
Keeping the criminal justice system at arm's length or otherwise rendering ineffective its activities is important for the survival of organized crime. A mixture of bribery and threats of violence against police or judicial personnel may be attempted, depending on the relative balance of power between the two institutions. At the lower levels of small-time organized crime police officers may be periodically found who are prepared to accept bribes and even participate in the planning of criminal actions. In Britain in the early 1980s the 'Operation Countryman' investigations showed something of the extent of police involvement in such relations even in a country with a relative lack of a tradition of state corruption and clientelism (Doig, 1984). On a more organized level powerful criminal groups may attempt to mix bribery with the threat of violence or assassination. The process is by no means unknown in Western Europe in which police officers and prosecutors – and on occasion even journalists pursuing organized crime – operate under conditions of threats and assassinations.

Even if the criminal justice system cannot be terrorized into inactivity it may be possible for criminal organizations to enter into various sorts of collusion. On an individual level an offender, once caught, may be granted immunity from prosecution in return for information leading to the successful prosecution of others. Such is the case with much organized crime and political terrorism. Periodic 'confessions' by Mafia notables, by no means all of it producing reliable evidence, are a constant feature of the 'war on organized crime' in both the United States and Italy. However it is the possibility of collusion between the criminal organization and elements of the criminal justice system with the aim of securing the continuity of criminal activity which is of importance here. On occasion governments may deliberately pursue a policy of collusion with criminal groups. The latter may for example be able to provide a supplement to state agencies in the maintenance of a particular political regime of 'law and order'. Some Latin American regimes in recent years have openly tolerated the existence of right-wing paramilitary murder squads as a form of control of left-wing political movements. States may turn a blind eye to the use by employers of criminal gangs as strike breakers, etc. The possibility of such an alliance and its degree of openness depends on the balance of political and social forces. Governments may miscalculate the political situation and find their collusion with criminal groups an embarrassment. It is currently a matter of some embarrassment to the United States government that, as the 'Irangate' hearings have revealed, US clandestine operations in the early 1980s aimed at supplying the Nicaraguan contras for armed struggle against the government of that country involved a close relationship with drug traffickers, in which US-financed aircraft taking illegal arms to the rebels were used for drug shipments on the return flight. Older examples of such collusion can be found in European history as in the years immediately following Italian unification, in which the central government whose power in Sicily and the south was still weak allowed the Mafia to act as an unofficial agency of law and order (Arlacchi, 1988).

The final avenue open to offenders is to secure the decriminalization of their activity. Offender groups generally do not have the collective political power to influence their decriminalization except as part of a wider social movement. Decriminalization of homosexual intercourse between consenting adults required a significant liberalization of public opinion in general for its achievement. Drug users are a particularly powerless group. However, socially powerful groups such as corporate capital may well be consulted by governments in the precess of legislation and thereby be able to influence the formulation of law to their advantage, even being able to engage in 'anticipatory decriminalization'. Organized crime has a much more ambiguous attitude to decriminalization since much of the vast profits to be made by trade in illegal commodities depends on the very situation of illegality. Consequently a more sophisticated form of 'decriminalization' is that in which the profits of illegal enterprise can be ploughed into safer forms of legitimate investment through sophisticated 'laundering' procedures (Taylor, 1989; Santino, 1989).

The reaction of victims to the state – as opposed to direct action by victims against offenders – is generally to the perceived inactivity of the latter. An exception is where the state itself is seen as the offender and where the relatives of those directly victimized by the state attempt to attract political support from wider social groups, from abroad or from subsequent governments to prosecute members of predecessor regimes. The activity of victim groups pressing increased activity and resources from the criminal justice system is often closely allied with movements to widen the boundaries of criminalization itself. The key variable is the extent to which wider groups in society will identify with the form of victimization in question. This is governed by the factors concerning the visibility and directness of victimization, the status of the victims in society, etc, as already discussed. Victim groups are at their most effective when they can become seen as the exemplary case of a wider social issue. Thus rape victims have in recent years benefited from a generalized support from the women's movement, which was instrumental in setting up rape crisis centres and mounting campaigns for changes in police and judicial treatment of rape, and which saw the treatment of such victims as epitomizing the generalized treatment of women in modern society. They may be contrasted with the poor and elderly victims of street mugging who during much of the same period found that the seriousness of their victimization was being loudly contested by radical groups and being denounced as media-orchestrated 'moral panic', or the powerless victims of corporate crime killings such as Bhopal who still many years after the event still await adequate compensation.

Conclusion

Most of the topics touched on in this chapter could be, and are, the subjects of lengthy studies in themselves. The aim here has been deliberately eclectic: to show that the development of criminology has to proceed concretely and synthetically by bringing a wide range of different factors together in the analysis of particular situations rather than developing one-sided generalized theories of 'the causes of crime' or 'the causes of criminalization'. The framework of the square of crime developed by left realism forces us to approach seemingly simple questions like 'why has crime risen over the last decade?' as the process of a complex structure of interactions. The task now is to demonstrate the utility of this framework in the concrete analysis of different types of criminality and policies aimed at controlling it.

Notes

1. Except rhetorically that is. 'A philosopher produces ideas, a poet verses, a parson sermons, a professor text books, etc. A criminal produces crime. The criminal produces not only crime but also the criminal law: he produces the professor who delivers lectures on this criminal law, and even the inevitable text books in which the professor presents his lectures as a commodity for sale in the market. . . . Further the criminal produces the whole apparatus of the police and criminal justice, detectives, judges, executioners . . .' (Marx, cited in Bottomore and Rubel, 1962).

2. Radical feminists who wish to assert with Dworkin that 'The annihilation of a woman's personality, individuality, will, character is prerequisite to male sexuality' (Dworkin, 1988) and that any man in any situation is as likely as any other to rape have to make recourse to ever-widening and blurring boundaries in the notion of sexual violence. Box himself was guilty of this (see 1983: 121–9; Kelly 1988).

3. The concept of marginality can end up as identical with relative deprivation in the sense that any group with blocked access to legitimate means of goal attainment is by definition marginalized. The only coherent use of the term is therefore as a reference to blocked access to those legitimate political processes such as trade unions, pressure groups, political parties, etc, which provide collective means to open up new channels for the achievement of legitimate goals or secure welfare compensation for those who have no access to existing means.

4. For example some feminist commentators on the Yorkshire Ripper murders in Britain have argued that it was only when the victims were no longer prostitutes but began to include 'respectable women' that the level of public outrage and the activities of the police were really galvanized into action (Ward-Jouve, 1987; Cameron and Frazer, 1987).

5. This is a separate question from the legal arguments concerning negligence and matters in which the offender is constrained to take responsibility for negligence. Indeed a good part of the legal prosecution of this type of crime consists precisely in the attribution of criminal responsibility for 'unintended' actions as when a large corporation is successfully penalized for environmental damage or ignoring safety procedures – in the hope that no deaths would occur – which have in fact resulted in death. At the time of writing British legal history is being made by the decision to criminally prosecute the owners of the ferry company whose alleged negligence resulted in the sinking of a vessel with the deaths of over 100 passengers at Zeebrugge in 1987.

References

Arlacchi, P. (1987) 'La questione criminale in Italia', in P. Arlacchi and N. della Chiesa (eds), *La Palude e la Citta*. Milan: Arnaldo Mondatori Editore.

Arlacchi, P. (1988) *Mafia Business*. Oxford: Oxford University Press.

Becker, G. (1968) 'Crime and punishment: an economic approach', *Journal of Political Economy*, 76: 169–217.

Bottomore, T. and Rubel, M. (eds) (1962) *Karl Marx: Selected Writings in Sociology and Social Philosophy*. Harmondsworth: Penguin.

Box, S. (1983) *Crime, Power and Mystification*. London: Tavistock.

Braithwaite, J. (1984) *Corporate Crime in the Pharmaceutical Industry*. London: Routledge and Kegan Paul.

Braithwaite, J. (1989) *Crime, Shame and Reintegration*. Cambridge: Cambridge University Press.

Cameron, D. and Frazer, L. (1987) *The Lust to Kill*. London: Polity Press.

Catanzaro, R. (1988) *Il Delitto Come Impresa: Storia Sociale della Mafia*. Padua: Liviana.

Chambliss, W. (1989) 'State organized crime', *Criminology*, 27(2): 183–207.

Clarke, M. (ed.) (1983) *Corruption*. London: Frances Pinter.

Cloward, R. and Ohlin, L. (1960) *Delinquency and Opportunity*. New York: Free Press.

Cohen, S. (1985) *Visions of Social Control*. London: Polity Press.

Cohen, L. and Felson, M. (1979) 'Social change and crime rate trends: a routine activity approach', *American Sociological Review*, 44, August: 588–608.

Coleman, A. (1986) *Utopia on Trial: Vision and Reality in Planned Housing*. London: Hilary Shipman.

Cook, J. (1980) 'Criminal deterrence: laying the groundwork for the second decade', in M. Tonry and N. Morris (eds), *Crime and Justice: An Annual Review*. Chicago: University of Chicago Press.

· Cullen, F., Maakestaad, J. and Cavender, G. (1987) *Corporate Crime under Attack: The Ford Pinto Case and Beyond.* Cincinnati: Anderson.

Davis, M. (1988) 'Los Angeles: civil liberties between the hammer and the rock', *New Left Review*, 170: 37–60.

de Leo, G. (1987) 'Il crimine come problema e la sua spiegazione: nuovo realismo e oltre', *Dei Delitti e Delle Pene*, IV(3): 453–67.

Doig, A. (1984) *Corruption*. London: Penguin Books.

Dworkin, A. (1988) *Intercourse*. London: Arrow Books.

Hall, S., Jefferson, T., Clarke, J. and Chritcher, C. (1976) *Policing the Crisis: Mugging, the State and Law and Order*. London: Macmillan.

Hess, H. (1973) *Mafia and Mafiosi: The Structure of Power*. Saxon House/Lexington Books.

Hulsman, L. (1986) 'Critical criminology and the concept of crime', *Contemporary Crisis*, 10: 63–80.

Jacobs, J. (1962) *The Death and Life of Great American Cities*. Harmondsworth: Penguin Books.

Johnson, K. (1986) 'Federal court processing of corporate, white collar, and common crime economic offenders over the past three decades', *Mid-American Review of Sociology*, 11(1): 25–44.

Jones, T. (1988) *Corporate Killing: Bhopals Will Happen*. London: Free Association Books.

Kelly, L. (1988) *Surviving Sexual Violence*. London: Routledge.

Kinsey, R., Lea, J. and Young, J. (1986) *Losing the Fight against Crime*. Oxford: Blackwell.

Lea, J. (1986) *Towards Social Prevention: The Crisis in Crime Prevention Strategy*. Middlesex Polytechnic: Centre for Criminology.

Lea, J. and Young, J. (1984) *What is to be Done about Law and Order?* Harmondsworth: Penguin Books.

Lemert, E. (1967) *Human Deviance: Social Problems and Social Control*. Englewood Cliffs: Prentice-Hall.

Levi, M. (1987) *Regulating Fraud: White Collar Crime and the Criminal Process*. London: Tavistock.

LRET (1986) *Neighbourhood Watch: Policing the Public*. London: Libertarian Research and Educational Trust.

Matthews, R. (1988) *Informal Justice?* London: Sage.

Merton, R. (1983) *Social Theory and Social Structure*. New York: Free Press.

Newman, K. (1983) *Report of the Commissioner of Police of the Metropolis*. London: HMSO.

Newman, O. (1972) *Defensible Space*. New York: Macmillan.

Passas, N. (1990) 'Anomie and corporate deviance', *Contemporary Crises*, 14(2): 158–72.

Pearce, F. (1976) *Crimes of the Powerful*. London: Pluto Press.

Pitch, T. (1987) 'Viaggio attorno alla "criminologia": Discutendo con i realisti', *Dei Delitti e Delle Pene*, IV(3): 469–89.

Rosenbaum, D. (1987) 'The theory and research behind neighbourhood watch: is it a sound fear and crime reduction strategy?', *Crime and Delinquency*, 33(1): 103–34.

Santino, U. (1989) 'The financial Mafia: the illegal accumulation of wealth and the financial–industrial complex', *Contemporary Crises*, 12: 203–43.

Santos, B. (1980) 'Popular justice, dual power and socialist strategy', in B. Fine (eds), *Capitalism and the Rule of Law*. London: Hutchinson.

Solivetti, L. (1987) 'La criminalita di impresa: alcuni commenti sul problema delle cause', *Sociologia del Diritto*, 14(1): 41–77.

Taylor, I. (1989) *Money Laundering and the Free Market Economy: A Report to the Research Division of the Ministry of the Solicitor General of Canada*. Ottawa: Carleton University.

Ward-Jouve, M. (1986) *The Streetcleaner: The Yorkshire Ripper Case on Trial*. London: Marion Boyars.

Warr, M. (1985) 'Fear of rape among urban women', *Social Problems*, 32(3): 238–50.

Wilson, J.Q. (1983) *Thinking about Crime* (2nd edn). New York: Vintage Books.

Wright, P. (1987) *Spycatcher*. New York: Viking Books.

Young, J. (1971) 'The police and the amplification of deviancy', in S. Cohen (ed.), *Images of Deviance*. Harmondsworth: Penguin Books.

Young, J. (1986) 'The failure of criminology: the need for a radical realism', in R. Matthews and J. Young (eds), *Confronting Crime*. London: Sage.

Young, J. (1987) 'The tasks facing a realist criminology', *Contemporary Crises*, 11: 337–56.

4 Left realist criminology and the free market experiment in Britain

Ian Taylor

England's in pieces. England's an old twat in the sea. England's cruel. My town's scruffed out. My people's pale. Pale face. Bang, bang, bang. It's a shoot-out with the sheriff. EDDIE, EDDIE, EDDIE, the hero. Don't weaken, or you're Dole and Done, Dole and Done, never weaken, show yourself sharp, so sharp you cut. Head Up. Eyes heard. Walk like Robert Mitchum.... Bang, Bang, Bang, Bang, Bang, Bang, Bang.

Everything's soiled you know, our house, me mum, the bath. I'm sick. Nowt's nice around me. Nowt's nice. NOWT'S NICE. Where's finery? Fucked off! Where soft? Gone hard. I want a walk on the mild side. I want to be clean. Cleaned. Spray me with something sweet, spray me away. (Cartwright, 1986)[1]

One of the most striking features of left realist criminology is the fact that it has developed into a significant 'school' or paradigm of criminology almost only in Britain.[2] Given also the fact that the key left realist papers and texts date from about 1981–2, it seems clear that left realist criminology ought to be understood primarily as a reaction on the part of some sections of the socialist academy in Britain to the general experience of Thatcherism and, in particular, as a response to the popularization of law-and-order policies by the Thatcher government, especially in its first two periods in office.[3] It can also be understood, we would argue, as a reaction on the part of some sections of the left to the 'summer riots' of 1980 and, in particular, of 1981 – the street confrontations between police and residents of Britain's inner cities which were quite without precedent, especially in the levels of violence that were involved, in the whole of twentieth-century British history.

I will be wanting, here, to read left realist criminology in part in its own terms, and, in particular, in terms of its connected concerns to take seriously the street crime and interpersonal and property crime that most intimately and destructively cuts into the lives of already disadvantaged, working-class people, and also in terms of its ongoing concern to advance a set of realistic crime control policies that could not only win support for the oppositional Labour Party but could also be adopted, in short order, by a newly elected Labour government. However, I also want to advance a reading of left realist criminology as being a *particular kind of meditation* on the conditions of social disorder in Britain in the 1980s and, therefore, as subsuming a particular and indeed controversial set of assumptions about the ways in which a generalized condition of social order might be prescribed and/or established in Britain. For the purpose of this particular chapter, my quizzical comments can be organized around six distinct areas of concern:

1 Left realism's celebration of the popular demand for crime control.
2 Left realism and the commonsense conception of 'crime'.
3 Left realism and the issue of class.
4 Left realism and the 'reinvention of criminology'.
5 Left realism and its conception of social disorder in a free market society.
6 Left realism and its idea of a 'minimalist' state.

I am aware that other urgent critiques of left realist criminology have already emerged, particularly from the direction of libertarian criminology – in respect of what is seen to be the left realists' 'regression' to the use of penal law as a means of social control (cf. Cohen, 1986). There has also been a quite angry series of critical responses to left realist criminology from scholars and activists in Britain who are identified with the vanguard organizations of the black underclass, and for whom left realist criminology is understood, overwhelmingly, as an outrageous accommodation to the law and order policies of a racist 'authoritarian state' (Gilroy and Sim, 1985; Scraton, 1987). And, finally, there has been criticism of left realist criminology on the specific grounds of its apparent acceptance of popular fear of crime and its subsequent adoption of a crime control strategy: a criticism that is mounted from a perspective which continues to insist on the exaggerated character of popular fears and which also insists on viewing the widely reported increased 'fear of crime' as an *ideological displacement* of the ongoing increases in *other* personal troubles (unemployment, race conflict, tensions between the sexes in 'late capitalist societies', etc) (Steinert, 1985; Hulsman, 1986). There may be some echoes of each of these sets of critical concerns (especially the last mentioned) in the commentary I want to advance here, but I do want to try and develop this commentary on left realism from a vantage point which accepts the critique advanced by left realists of the abstentionism of many left intellectuals vis-a-vis the project of bringing about a restoration of lived social order in Britain, and which tries indeed to develop a specifically social-democratic solution to the problem of *social disorder*.

Left realism and the popular demand for crime control

One of the most insistent refrains in the writing of left realist criminologists in Britain has been that the social-democratic left, if ever it is to be seen as attending to popular needs and anxieties, must 'take crime seriously'. So much of the work of left realists, discussed elsewhere in this volume, and in Matthews and Young (1992), has focused on the measurement of criminal victimization and the popular fear of crime (Jones et al., 1986), and has also been concerned with the neighbourhood crime prevention schemes (especially in highly stressed multiply deprived working-class and ethnic areas such as the Broadwater Farm Estate), and, perhaps even more controversially, with the attempt to intervene in the current direction of development of British policing (Kinsey et al., 1986). A closely connected but relatively underdeveloped argument in left realism has been on the need for the left to develop a coherent perspective and strategy with respect to the punishment and correction of offenders. The connected thrusts of this left realist argument (which has so far been developed only very tentatively and unevenly) are, on the one hand, to argue for the protection of communities from criminal behaviours by the pursuit of policies of 'pre-emptive deterrence' while, on the other, to argue for a minimalist use of prison, 'only . . . in circumstances where there is extreme danger to the community' (Lea and Young, 1984: 267).

It is beyond the scope of this chapter to discuss the detail of this social-democratic programme of crime prevention and police reform. What concerns us more here is the overall *political and theoretical effect* of the left realists' accommodation to – and indeed their construction of – the popular fear about crime and the associated popular demand for social control and 'order'.

Left realists consistently claim to be speaking for and on behalf of 'the people', and also to be speaking in the tradition of a realistically minded social democratic politics, which itself resonates in and throughout the popular consciousness. But, on the first point, it does have to be said that the evidence presented in the various victimization studies conducted by left realists has more to do with patterns of victimization and of fear than it has to do with any detailed, careful excavation of popular consciousness with respect to questions of deterrence, coercive punishment and/or social policies as answers to crime and social order. There is no really creative attempt in the survey work of the left realists to investigate the *range* of popular sentiment(s) that might be found in the population with respect to the ways and means of combating crime, or of restoring some sense of order, in dislocated inner-city neighbourhoods or in downtown city centres.

The truth is, of course, that social democratic scholars and political activists have argued throughout most of this century that the solutions to problems of crime and social disorder are predominantly social and economic rather than penal. Echoes and variants of these positions are distributed throughout the population, presenting themselves in different forms and 'mixes' in different historical circumstances.

To argue that *particular kinds* of social and economic strategy (like post-war Keynesianism) no longer work as means of maintaining social order or keeping down crime is in no way to indict the potential of social and economic strategies *in general*, and certainly does not provide the warrant for speaking as if penal law could ever establish the *social conditions* in which a sense of social order could be generalized throughout a whole society. It is important not to forget that the early post-war period of 'Fabian' social reconstruction in Britain – at least until the mid-1950s – *was* a period in which commentators did speak of an overwhelming sense of order and stability (born of the hopes that were popularly held of a New Jerusalem, with respect to access to decent housing, education, health services and social welfare). And, to connect to our earlier historicist argument, it was also, if surviving survey data are to be believed, a period in which the 'popular consciousness' was not predominantly articulated around a demand for the more repressive application of criminal law as a solution to immediate social and criminal problems. Support for the retention of capital punishment, for example, declined significantly within the British population from the late 1940s (with only 25 percent opposing it in 1947) to the mid-1950s, when there was widespread unease about the execution of murderers (cf. Christoph, 1962: 43). In the United States, in 1966, there was actually a majority against capital punishment (47 percent against, and 41 percent for): a massive shift of public opinion compared with the figures reported for 1953 (68 percent for capital punishment, 25 percent against it). It is clearly important to try and understand the social 'conditions of existence' of these radical shifts in public sentiment with respect to capital punishment in the United States and in Britain and their importance in the maintenance of a sense of public order, and to compare the conditions underlying these shifts with conditions obtaining in other societies.

Left realists have been very dismissive of the role of 'high theory' in British radical criminology, but it is surely no theoretical abstraction, especially for social democratic thinkers interested in arguing for alternative forms of social organization, to insist on the close relationship between economic and social conditions (and, therefore, on the direction and efficacy of government economic and social policy) and the 'shape' of popular consciousness with respect to the control of social dislocation and crime.

Left realism and the commonsense conception of crime

In the early 1980s, in particular, and more so in the aftermath of the riots of 1981, left realists were insistent that the problem of street crime was absolutely central to popular consciousness about crime and, therefore, a vital issue in the left's response to a popular common sense about crime. This assertion was underlined by a series of critical, quite dismissive references to the lack of interest on the part of what the left realists categorized as 'left idealist criminology' (from the late 1960s to the early 1980s) with respect to the crimes committed against working-class people and, indeed, a lack of interest therefore in *real crime*: '. . . frequently, left idealism simply ignores crime as a problem of any significance. Disorder remains central to the study of society – left idealism has, at least, achieved that aim of radical criminology. But it is disorder purged of crime' (Matthews and Young, 1986: 17).

Left realists have also justified their heavy focus on street crime as a reflection of the 'remarkable degree of reported agreement throughout the population over the "problem" of crime' (Matthews, 1987: 380). But very little evidence is provided in support of these assertions and no curiosity is evident as to whether such a degree of consensus, if true, is actually a cultural phenomenon of the present, or some kind of cultural universal. A survey of British public opinion on crime, conducted for the BBC in conjunction with a television series *On Crime* in 1960, found very significant differences between 'working-class' and 'middle-class' respondents as to their views on the most serious of crimes and their views about crime reduction. For 'working-class' respondents, the worst crimes were indecent assault and cruelty to children, followed by murder, but for 'middle-class' respondents, the worst crime was 'planned murder for money' (BBC, 1961, Part I, Table VII: 15). It would appear from these figures that the popular consensus which left realists say exist about crime was only (in 1960) true at the level of generalization around the signifying word 'crime': the degree of *substantive* consensus around what constitutes really serious anti-social or disorderly behaviour was far less clear.

In accommodating to the idea of street crime as 'real crime', therefore, left *realism* is actually constructing a *theoretical* description in which 'crime' and 'social disorder' are very closely linked. It is true that left realists do distinguish their position on the 'crime–social disorder connection' from that of right realists, by insisting that crime: 'is a result of the fundamental structural problems of capitalism. It relates to all these problems; it is not separate from them'. But they do also concur with right realists about the problems that are caused *by* crime, especially for working-class people. Crime can be a *compounding cause*, in the left realist view, in the generalized emergence of quiescence, resignation or even despair in working-class neighbourhoods. So crime is a *cause* of problems that could be significantly reduced or alleviated by corrective or determined action against crime, including, quite definitely, a visible, effective official police force, especially at the neighbourhood level.

A central problem with this perspective as to the problems that are *caused by crime* is the rather formal reliance, in the theoretical account that is being provided of disorder in civil society, on the concept of 'crime' and the relationships between 'crime' and other aspects of the broader social environment. Precisely the same problem obtains, it should be said, in the much-quoted 'right realist' article – 'Broken windows' – on vandalism and public space by Wilson and Kelling (1982), to which the left realists give quite extensive attention.

The truth, as the left realists note themselves elsewhere in their writing, is that the sense of personal fear and insecurity that is widely reported in victim studies is a patterned and highly localized fear, most obvious and evident in inner-city neighbourhoods and in particular downtown or city centre 'environments' (underground walkways, tunnels, etc). The sense of personal insecurity, therefore, is a tangible expression of the interpersonal and social consequences of building overcrowded, cheap and poorly designed public housing for the housing of underclass people, on the one hand, and, on the other, the destruction of a sense of public space in city centres brought about by poor urban planning and by the absence (or exhaustion) of the sense of civic pride and imagination on the part of British city councils – especially during the 1960s and 1970s.

To make this point is not to reiterate Heinz Steinert's attempt to replace the talk of 'crime' altogether by talk of 'troubles', 'conflicts' and 'difficulties' (Steinert, 1985: 329). It is, instead, to point to the inescapable political and policy implications and importance of the concepts and framework through which one identifies the object of analysis in *any* kind of talk about social disorder. To interpret or understand the findings of *The British Crime Survey* or the Islington or Merseyside Victims Surveys as expressions of a deep, popular recognition of *a decline of levels of public care and public provision* (with respect, for example, to the design or maintenance of public housing or the architecture of the downtown core) is to think towards archi-

-tectural, social and economic, rather than penal, conclusions about the means and ways of restoring 'order' in those communities.

It is of some significance to our argument here to compare British crime prevention programmes (with their heavy reliance on policing, neighbourhood watch and the fortification of private space) with the programmes that have been developed in France, in the aftermath of the Bonnemaison Commission Report of 1982. Some 480 local crime prevention councils have apparently been established in France since 1982, coordinating the work of social workers, the judiciary and voluntary agencies at the level of the neighbourhood, but also obtaining the input of the citizens as to their views on crime control in their own locality. The end result in many cases has been a major programme of renovation of run-down and dilapidated housing estates, coupled with the creation of a network of *missions locales* (whose mandate apparently is to guide young people into 'adult life and secure work'). Where crime *is* committed, it is dealt with by *ilotiers* (akin to the famous, but now non-existent, British bobby – neighbourhood beat police officers who focus on everyday problems such as fights and bag-snatchers; and there are also highly developed schemes, in cities like Toulouse, for mediation between offenders and victims (cf. Boseley, 1987). Generally speaking, there is a much heavier emphasis on the power of a reorganized, and indeed a 're-moralized', community of citizens in the reduction of disorder than there is reliance on conventional police either as crime-fighters themselves or as an impersonal embodiment of an idea of 'community'.

Many commentators believe that the Bonnemaison crime prevention schemes are the major factor in the significant recent declines in the rate of reported crime in France: having increased alarmingly by 21.6 percent in 1981–2, crime rates have declined steadily every year since and, in 1985–6, dipped sharply by over 8 percent.

Our concern here is not to attack the left realists for their attempt to focus on a social democratic police strategy or penal policy. But it is to try to tease out the policy and political implications of trying to think the problem of social disorder in contemporary Britain exclusively and/or primarily through the commonsensical – and indeed conventionally criminological – concept of 'crime' and the 'causal' relationships between 'crime' and the broader environment.

The left realist school has, indeed, begun to move away from an exclusive focus on mugging, thefts and other forms of street crime as the prime object of analysis of its criminology. The victimization surveys completed in Islington, for example, highlighted the extraordinary importance of sexual assaults in the 'fear of crime' exhibited by Islington women of all age groups and races, and reported a higher rate of sexual assault in Islington than was found by the *British Crime*

Survey. It seems likely, for all kinds of reasons, that the continuing increases in the numbers of assaults and rapes is a function, not only of changes in police practice with respect to the recording and treatment of offences against women, but also a function of the real stresses and strains in the relations of the sexes in contemporary Britain. We have only to mention the incidents at Hungerford in 1987, and in Düsseldorf and other German towns during the European Soccer Championships in 1988, to draw attention to the troubled and pressing condition of traditional British masculinity. We do not pretend to be able to theorize this issue here (cf. for a useful attempt at this kind of analysis, Seabrook, 1987) but we do think it is very important in any understanding of the popular sense of disorder and insecurity in British city centres and the inner city – most recently, for example, in respect of the growth of public drinking on buses, the London Underground or in city centre shopping malls (cf. Bradley, 1988).

We cannot even begin to speculate here on the relationship between this crisis of masculinity and the rapidly increasing rates of child sexual abuse which have been reported in Britain, although, with MacLeod and Saraga (1988), we *would* want to assume that the abuse is, at some level, a reflection of the conventional and patriarchal view of the family as existing to satisfy the emotional and sexual needs of men. So we do say that sexual abuse and assault, whether on the street or in domestic and other private spheres, is at root a problem to do with the crisis of traditional masculinity, which finds its expression in all kinds of other forms of public and private violence. But it really is not clear that the problem of masculinity is a problem that is specifically and clearly identified, *conceptually or prescriptively*, in left realist criminology, where the discussion of 'crimes against women' is organized as if these behaviours are primarily to be understood as exemplars and vindications of the left realists' emphasis on 'crime in the streets'.

Nor is it clear what the left realist position might be, conceptually and politically, with respect to the rapid increase in hard drug use, particularly heroin, notably among British youth in the larger urban areas (cf. Pearson, 1988; Parker, 1988). There is no doubt that the increasing popularity of hard drugs is closely linked to some of the reported increases in property crime and theft, but it is not at all clear whether there is any effective policy for the control of drug use based on ideas of punishment or deterrence. It is not clear either what attitudes are enshrined in 'popular consciousness' with respect to drug use, and whether the drug problem *is* seen by 'working people' as a criminal problem, or alternatively as a pressing welfare problem or, indeed, as evidence of the need for a radical redirection of national economic and social priorities, especially with respect to youth.

We want, finally in this section, to anticipate the later development of our argument, by pointing to the extraordinary explosion of concern in Britain in early 1987 and again during the summer of 1988 over an apparently new criminal phenomenon of so-called 'rural violence'. This particular panic over crime was a reaction of police and local residents in the Home Counties to the drunkenness and inter-personal violence displayed, before and after 'closing time' in public houses, by the new rich who have bought houses in rural villages and towns across the south-east of England. In mass media and public discussion, these new forms of anti-social behaviour were powerfully signified by reference to the figure of 'Loadsamoney', a character created by Harry Enfield on a late night Channel Four television show, as a satire on the kind of morality that is said to have been produced by 'Thatcherism', especially among young men employed in the financial services industry. Once again, we have to say that the significance of the new, middle-class, rural crime is simply not confronted, con-ceptually and/or politically, by a realism that remains committed to the stubbornly empirical object-of-analysis of street crime. We may begin to think, indeed, that the 'realism' of left realist criminology is akin to some other forms of traditional social democratic thinking, in its resurrection, *in too one-sided a way*, of the realities of a declining working class and its failure to connect, 'realistically' or imaginatively, to the transformations in the form of patriarchy, the family or the disorderly pastimes of the new middle class.

Left realism and the issue of class

The direction of recent political and economic developments in Britain, and in other late capitalist societies, has been forcing many socialist and social democratic commentators to confront very carefully and systematically the continuing utility of 'class analysis' and, indeed, of a politics based on some notion of a unitary class interest.

Some of the commentators who have ventured into this territory – noting in particular the decline in numbers of the traditional industrial working class in all developed capitalist societies – have begun to speak of the *disappearance* of the working class as such (Gorz, 1982; Laclau and Mouffe, 1985). Other analytical commentators, rather more care-fully, have been paying close attention to the particular *recomposition* that the working class has been undergoing over the last decade. Charles Leadbeater (1987), for example, tries to develop a typology of the British workforce in the late 1980s, based on the types of employ-ment and/or unemployment that are being experienced: he identifies the six distinct groups of (1) the long-term unemployed, (2) the recurrently unemployed, (3) the rapidly increasing 'army of peripheral workers, part-timers, free-lancers, temporary workers and self-employed' (Leadbeater 1987: 2), (4) the semi-skilled and unskilled full-time workers, (5) the skilled 'core workers' and (6) the managers, directors, stockbrokers and bankers, all of whom have enjoyed enormous gains in the last decade. He also points, with many other commentators, to the enormous divisions that have opened up in the differences of wealth and security between different regions of the UK, as well as within particular regions. So while it is true that the south-east of England is generally more prosperous than the north, it is also the case that certain areas in the north are much more prosperous than either Hackney in East London or Moss Side in Manchester.

Leadbeater does not press the point as much as he should, but it is also very much the case that this process of recomposition of the working class has had momentous effects on women and on members of Britain's sizeable immigration and visible minority population. Quite disproportionate numbers of women are concentrated into Leadbeater's 'army' of peripheral and part-time workers, and absolutely disproportionate numbers of West Indian people, especially West Indian youth, are unemployed either recurrently or on a very long-term basis, with occasional forays into unskilled or semi-skilled employment.

It is not our concern in this chapter to enter directly into the angry debate which has been provoked by the left realists' writings on 'race and crime.' But it is important to understand the particular approach to 'class' and 'marginality' adopted by the left realists, and then the application of this structural account of subcultural theory as a means of explaining differential crime rates. The left realists have adopted the analysis of class formation and social stability associated with theorists like Ralf Dahrendorf (1985) and Gianfranco Poggi (1978). In this account, three distinct stages are identified in the patterns of class formation and social order and disorder. The eighteenth and nine-teenty centuries are identified as a period of considerable collective violence associated with the resistance of an artisan class to the discipline of industrial capitalism. The second stage, in the nineteenth century and beyond, involved the gradual incorporation of the masses into the organized industrial process and also into the organized political processes (most notably through the extension of the franchise). A crucial role in the successful incorporation of the enlarged industrial working class was played by the political parties which were formed to represent labour in parliamentary and local government assemblies, as well as by the trades unions which were established and allowed to negotiate with capital on behalf of organized labour. The left realists observe with respect to this second stage that:

> It is not our purpose here to criticize or evaluate this system of politics, just

to point out that this political system was, historically, associated with the means by which violence was replaced by a process of political compromise ... in the relations between the two main classes of workers and employers. (Lea and Young, 1984: 203)

Lea and Young recognize that this compromise is 'by no means immune from occasional resource to violence' (p. 204) but they do emphasize that this compromise was more and more effectively protected and institutionalized throughout the twentieth century by the routine political compromises and settlements taking place in Parliament as well as by the process of economic negotiation engaged in by trades unions and employers. This great compromise of capital and labour, and of the organized power of the bourgeois state with the masses, was the guarantee, according to left realists, of a certain degree of predictability and order in everyday economic and social relations.

In the late twentieth century, however, Lea and Young want to suggest, this process of political and class compromise (and the reproduction of social order) has been significantly impeded, in particular, by the development of micro-technology and by the effects this has had in 'expelling' people from the process of production. In this third stage:

> ... we are witnessing ... the growth of a generation of young people in our inner cities and decaying industrial areas whose contact with the work process is, if existent at all, minimal and peripheral ... (the) marginalization of these young people from the process of production means marginalization from the process of interest-group formation and political compromise which we have described as a crucial stabilizing feature of democratic political systems. (Lea and Young, 1984: 208)

So the general structural conditions making for a breakdown of the kind of orderly and predictable social and economic relations of the period of the Great Compromise are the crisis of unemployment and, in particular, the emergence of an ever-increasing marginalized or underclass population. The different adaptations exhibited within this population to this structurally generated process of marginalization are, however, to be explained 'culturally' or, indeed, via the application of a subcultural theory. One of the most controversial aspects of left realist criminology has, indeed, been its use of subcultural theory as a way of explaining the differential adaptations of West Indian and Asian migrants to the experience of racial oppression and social and economic marginalization, and, in particular, as a means of explaining the criminal involvement of some segments of the West Indian or black minority population (cf. Bridges and Gilroy, 1982; Gilroy, 1982).

For our purposes here, it is also important to register that the left realists' accommodation to a generalized *sociological explanation of social order* during the period of the Great Compromise is controversial. It is by no means clear that the period of the Great Compromise ever amounted to more than a pale imitation of a fully fledged social democracy. Even more pragmatically, however, there are obvious problems of historical periodicization in the historical account thereby constructed – given, for example, that the rise in juvenile crime in Britain began in 1955 (long before the onset of mass youth unemployment). Other critical commentators would want to question the 'orderliness' (sic) of a period that included the Great Strike, the recession and mass unemployment and two world wars. So there are some serious issues in the rather generalized sociology of social order offered by Poggi and Dahrendorf, and adopted by left realism. The application of this analysis as a framework (without qualification) for explaining the crimes of ethnic minorities in Britain does construct the 'black British' as 'beyond and outside' the assumed and commonsensical notion of the 'working class' that resides in the left realists' texts. The black population is treated as if it is *almost by definition* a core member group in the marginalized population. The clear contrast is with the discussion of women in left realist texts. Left realists, referring in recent work to the 'profound contribution of feminist victimology' (Young, 1988: 301), *do* seem to write about women as if, by virtue of being victims of street crime and/or sexual assaults, they become honorary members of the core working class. Left realism appears to be distancing itself from 'black' movements, but simultaneously making a close identification with (a certain version of) feminism.

In moving so close both to a celebration of feminist victimology *and* the working-class family form, left realism also avoids discussion of the problem of patriarchy within the traditional working class and the potential for sexual violence, exploitation and abuse within the working-class family. And, in so doing, it also fails to see the prevalence of patriarchal power in the respectable, bourgeois family. It does not deal 'seriously', we may say – to appropriate a left realist use of terms – with the independent importance of patriarchy and sexual inequality across the social formation as a whole.

This is partly to say that left realists do not assign patriarchy its own, 'relatively autonomous' history, emerging in parallel to (but not in correspondence with) the history of the formation of class. It is also to suggest that they do not offer or appear to consider a careful history of race and ethnicity, or of patterns of immigration, in the British social formation. So there is a sense in left realist literature that the fact of immigration is new, and that it is historically coterminous with the process of dislocation associated with the decline of welfare state social democracy and the 'post-war settlement' from the late 1960s onwards.

The absence of a detailed historical consideration of the relationship between ethnicity and class formation does allow the assignation of the West Indian population primarily to the marginalized population, but it does not yield a sense of the real complexities in the relationship between class and ethnicity developing over time.

There is some sense of a recognition, in some recent left realist work, of the confusions and problems arising out of the attempt to theorize the question of social order entirely through a notion of 'class'. In his recent discursive set of theoretical reflections on left realism, for example, Roger Matthews observes – rather enigmatically – that:

> ... it might seem strange that although the problem of crime is framed predominantly in terms of *class* the organization of crime control tends to be couched mainly in terms of *community*. This shift is ... not the result of an accidental slippage or confusion of categories but seems to result from some ambiguity over *the class basis of the victim–offender relation* as well as problems related to the mobilization of crime control efforts. (Matthews, 1987: 385, emphasis added)

In an even more radical departure from the earlier statements of the left realist position, Matthews goes on to argue for making alliances with urban, cultural and other political movements within the city, although he insists that: 'The analysis of social movements is not designed to displace the significance of class analysis but rather to incorporate a wider set of power relations and to identify the varieties of collective action operating in contemporary "post-industrial" society' (Matthews, 1987: 392).

But the significance of social movements over and above 'the class' is only recognized and discussed as a part of the 'mobilization of community' against *crime*. The introduction of social relations over and above the working class itself is a way of giving healthy additional support to the fight against pathology, located in and around 'the working class' and destructive, above all, of the working class's own sense of solidarity and community. There is no serious attempt to try and identify the *many and various* kinds of *stressed social relations* as such that now go to make up the structured and complex totality that is British society, articulated, as these are, in and through inequalities of gender, race, position within the labour market, and position on the map of regional inequality, and *then* to analyse the relation of these different fractions of the social formation to fears and/or experiences of something they may call 'crime'. This is unfortunate, since the left realists' victimization work surely provided an ideal opportunity for them to investigate in some detail the patterned but differentiated character of popular consciousness with respect to offences like sexual assault and mugging and, indeed – as we shall argue later – to fraud, sharp practice and corruption; and then to connect this 'popular consciousness' to the closely related questions of urban neglect, public provision, government economic policy or, indeed, the moral character and direction of the broad society.

The discussion is *not* intended to be read, I should reaffirm, as a denial of the utility of class analysis, or a 'realist', 'class' position on crime. But it is intended to raise the proper sociological question of the early 1990s: what is the working class now? And can we speak of this complex, patterned and differentiated set of subordinate social groups, defined by their area of residence, the nature of their occupation or their unemployment, by their racial group membership and by their gender, as having a unitary orientation towards something called 'crime' and/or crime control? Might it not be equally pressing to *investigate* the particular kinds of discursive positions on questions like crime and its relationship to penal law and policing, and also social policy and 'social justice', that may be held to by specific 'fractions' of 'the class' and of the social formation in general?

Left realism and the reinvention of criminology

One of the more startling recent developments in British social scientific circles was the organization of a National Conference on Crime and Criminology, held at the University of Sheffield in the summer of 1987. This apparently very well-attended event was remarkable for the fact of giving space in one conference to an extraordinarily broad cross-section of criminological voices, from the most unreconstructed and unrepentant psychological positions, through symbolic interactionism and on into left realism itself. Many observers attending the conference have reported astonishment at what appeared to be a virtual suspension of the epistemological and political debate and conflict which has characterized British criminology since the late 1960s. These same observers have also reported being dismayed by the amnesia which many participants at this conference were apparently displaying with respect to the enormous theoretical attack which had been mounted over the previous 19 years on the idea of an autonomous professional discipline of 'criminology', characterized as this discipline previously had been by an inert adherence to positivist method and to 'correctionalism' applied to pathological individuals. As a discipline, it was also absolutely oblivious to the central role of social theory and philosophy in any focused and/or visionary appraisal of the problem of social disorder. But, in 1987, it was as if the immediate conditions of constraint and occupational insecurity that obtained in many higher educational institutions in Britain was provoking the *reinvention*, for the most pragmatic of reasons, of a professional and disciplinary concept of 'criminology'. And it was also as if the continuing escalation of crime rates in Britain, up by some 50 percent overall since the election of the Thatcher government in 1979, had generated the urgent, popular and political, demand *for* a criminology that *could* produce some practical and immediate answers.

Not the least important of the developments informing this reconstruction, or reinvention, of criminology in Britain has been the growth in the numbers of professionals who are employed specifically as criminologists. The largest body of criminologists employed in one institution is employed not within a university, but within the Home Office Research Unit in London. Many local city authorities also employ professional criminologists to advise on crime prevention programmes and policing. And there are also quite significant numbers of graduate criminologists employed in national organizations such as the National Association for the Care and Resettlement of Offenders and the Howard League for Penal Reform.

Jock Young has written of this development as 'the emergence of a new administrative criminology'. He suggests that the defining characteristic of 'administrative criminology' is that it sidesteps what he calls the 'aetiological crisis' (the failure of Fabian, welfare state liberalism as a post-war strategy, *inter alia*, for the reduction of crime). Administrative criminology avoids the large questions of political and social strategy altogether:

> ... by suggesting that the causes of crime are either relatively unimportant or politically impossible to tackle. There is no need to explain the rise in crime: it is obvious that there is a rise. Rather we must find ways of stemming its impact. The question becomes what is the most cost-effective way of making control interventions, an emphasis on the purely technical cost–benefit ratio aspects of crime: the opportunities for crime available in the environment and the high risks attached to criminal activity. (Rock and Downes, 1982, quoted in Young, 1988: 306)

The development of this very narrow and technical conception of the criminological task has provoked some protest from within established British criminology in the universities, but the left realist judgement is that administrative criminology has nonetheless achieved a hegemonic status, in the absence of any coherent alternative (especially with respect to questions of strategy and policy) within orthodox British criminology, whether inside the academy or among the ranks of other professional criminologists.

What is intriguing and controversial for our purposes is the position which left realism adopts with respect to the growth of administrative criminology and, implicitly thereby, to the reinvention of criminology. Having lambasted left idealist criminology for its self-deceiving refusal to take crime seriously and its eschewal of the popular demand for crime reduction and crime control, left realists insist that *the* real debate 'in the present period' is between administrative criminology and the competing 'radical' paradigm of left realist criminology:

> [These] two criminologies can not only influence each other but they are in debate over the interpretation of the data. Most importantly... they can agree that there are common data to argue about.... There is a measure of agreement that there is something out there at the end of the telescope which is not just a function of the instrument itself. (Young, 1988: 307)

The argument is that the debate *within* (sic) British criminology has moved from a position of 'incommensurability' (between left idealism and positivistic criminology) into a situation where there is 'genuine competition and incompatibility' between the radical, left realist, paradigm and administrative criminology.

But there are some curious features about this new situation: the agreed sets of data are, indeed, data about crime as defined 'officially' or 'commonsensically'. *This* is not a debate that is *primarily* constructed around the broad conditions, or the prerequisites, of *social order as such*: it is a debate about the appropriate interpretation of victimization and other crime data and the most effective means for the reduction of crime, especially within the inner city and in working-class neighbourhoods.

Another of the curious features of this left realist construction of the field, which seems to derive directly from its belief that 'the new administrative criminology' is now 'the major paradigm in establishment approaches to crime' (Young, 1988: 306), is its implicit disavowal of the overwhelming importance and influence of the moral and political rhetoric of the Conservative government itself on questions of law and order and crime. But the truth surely is that *the* dominant 'criminology' of the 1980s in Britain was the persistent and raucous authoritarian/moralism of the Thatcher government itself. This was a popular and populist criminology which had clearly broken with welfare-liberalism and particularly with the theories of individual rehabilitation and permissiveness as a response to crime and delinquency; it has been a criminology that proclaims its commitment to the control of those crimes (mugging, theft, street violence, vandalism) which are most common to 'ordinary people'; and it has also been a criminology which has argued, strongly, from the opening days of the 1979 election campaign onwards, for the enormously powerful deterrent potential of policing, on the one hand, and severe courtroom sentences, on the other. And as it has become apparent to all that this emphasis on policing and penal law as a solution to 'real crime' has not succeeded – as the crime rates have continued to increase (and crimes of violence, in particular, have escalated) – so the Thatcher government has carefully shifted the emphasis in its own rhetoric from an exclusive emphasis on the 'barrier of steel' (an enhanced police presence and a vigilant court system) – which characterized its talk between 1979 and 1982 – to a much more elaborated rhetoric concerned with the moral reconstruction of Britain.

The new campaign for the positioning of an unashamedly bourgeois morality at the core of civil society is most apparent in Britain in Education Secretary Kenneth Baker's campaign to reform, and undermine, the permissive and liberal form that has been assumed by state education since the mid- to late-1960s, and to reinstitute a system of education organized around a core curriculum and a set of educational 'standards' and/or 'attainment targets' (cf. Department of Education and Science, 1987). To these specific organizational proposals, however, have been added a series of additional moral disquisitions as to the crucial moral role of schools. In a series of speeches and articles throughout 1988, the Conservative Home Secretary, Douglas Hurd, has argued for the introduction of the teaching of personal, civic and parental responsibility into 'every aspect of school life' in order to counter what he describes as a growing 'moral brutishness' among teenagers (Hurd, 1988c). He has also spoken, in what came to be called the Tamworth Manifesto, of the need for the reactivation of the Victorian ideal of charitable and voluntary work, on the grounds that the achievement of a sense of moral and social order must involve 'inspiring and enlisting . . . the active citizen in all walks of life' (Hurd, 1988a). Without such exemplary moral leadership, Mr Hurd believes, there is no chance of restoring a sense of cohesion in Britain's inner cities or, indeed, in the smaller cities and market towns which have suffered disruption on the part of 'youths who were white, employed, affluent and drunk'. Without the emergence of such a voluntary commitment to neighbourhood and, specifically, to one's obligations as a citizen, then there is little chance of the restoration of social cohesion. In this vision of society, strongly contrasted to the left's alleged own image of citizenship as a series of rights, the obligations of individual citizens are said to be to 'family, neighbourhood and nation'. So the Conservative government is now busily engaged in devolving the power and responsibility for the organization and protection of moral order to 'smaller groups' and away from the 'corporatist batallions':

> Thus parents will gain a bigger say in education. Council tenants will get more control over the management of their estates. Local radio stations will multiply under our new policy. . . . I do not doubt that as our policy towards the National Health Service matures it will rely more on the loyalties which our local hospitals still attract. (Hurd, 1988b)

Tellingly, for the purposes of this argument, Mr Hurd makes it quite clear that the success of crime prevention policies based on some variant of the neighbourhood watch scheme *is absolutely dependent* on the creation in local neighbourhoods of a sense of moral responsibility for others (which is, self-evidently for Conservatives, a question of leadership and example). Crucially, this cannot be legislated, they argue, by the state.

Now it may be that social democrats will want to reject or significantly qualify the Conservatives' version of morality – undeniably, a *bourgeois* morality concerned to equate individual worth with the ownership of wealth and property (cf. Thatcher, 1988). But this would not impugn the fact that a moral and philosophical argument with some content, and with some diagnostic power and prescriptive purchase on the popular imagination, is now being insistently and persuasively articulated in Britain. Given the prominence of these arguments in Britain's increasingly conservative press, and given the regularity with which such moral arguments are advanced as responses to particular incidents of crime (like the Hungerford killings), it seems quite shortsighted for left realist analysis to claim that the hegemony within criminology has been decisively achieved by the technician-practitioners of 'administrative criminology'. Certainly, one of the most unfortunate effects of the characterization of the criminological debate in Britain as being conducted between left realism and administrative criminology is the *side-stepping* of the most difficult of all issues in contemporary Britain: confronting the force of 'new right' thinking across the broad range of moral issues and social policy, and offering a coherent and comprehensive alternative, and one which is capable of mobilizing the popular imagination.

Left realism and the free market

Over 80 years ago, in trying to make sense of the steep increases in crime, delinquency and a sense of social disorder in industrial Britain, consequent on the rise of Empire, rapid but extremely uneven increases in income and affluence, and the generalized expansion of commerce and finance, the utopian socialist thinker Edward Carpenter, observed that:

> feverish anxiety is the keynote of (the great mass of people's) lives. There is no room for natural gladness or buoyancy of spirits. You may walk the streets of our great cities, but you will hear no one singing – except for coppers; hardly a playboy today whistles in his furrow, and in almost every factory (this is a fact) if a workman sang at his work he would be 'sacked'. We are like shipwrecked folk clambering up a cliff. The waves are raging below. Each one clings by handhold or foothold where he may, and in the

panic if he push his neighbour from a point of vantage, it is to be regretted certainly, but it cannot be helped. (Carpenter, 1905: 24)

Carpenter was in no doubt as to the source and the potential consequences of the economic developments of his time:

> ... it must not be blinked that in the growth of the modern millionaire we are face to face with a serious evil. Now that any man endowed with a little low cunning, and tempted by self conceit and a love of power, has a good chance of making himself enormously rich, society is in great danger of being ruled by as mean a set of scoundrels as ever before in our history. And nothing less than a great transformation in our moral and social standards will enable us to cope with this danger. (Carpenter, 1905: 110)

Contemporary left realist criminology lays great store by its ability to *explain* crime (Young, 1987: 337). We have tried to show earlier in this chapter, however, that the chosen object-of-analysis of left realists is *street crime* rather than any broader definition of *social disorder*; and we have also tried to show that the left realists' criminological accounting rests on a sociological account of the incorporation of the working class into industrial life and political democracy during the late nineteenth and early twentieth centuries, and the threat that is now posed to the social order by the development of high technology and the rapid emergence of a marginalized and unemployed underclass. We have suggested that this account is too heavily and one-dimensionally preoccupied with the historical trajectory of class relations, and insufficiently attentive to the historical 'logic' of relations between the sexes and to the continuous history of immigration and ethnic conflict.

But we can also begin to see other, important limiting effects of the left realists' focus on street crime, and also their lack of real interest in the complex relationship between political economy and civil society. We are presented, very frequently, with an image of a reconstituted social formation in Britain comprising, on the one hand, the 'working people' in general and, on the other, the marginalized underclass. We have little sense of the stresses and strains, or the hopes, aspirations and, indeed, the desires of upwardly mobile fully employed workers caught up in the explosion of economic activity in the south east. There is no attempt, either, to analyse the range of contradictions that are opening up in this 'free market economy' (between the *promises* of fortune and leisure, and the *reality* of vastly extended work weeks and enormous increases in occupational insecurity). So very little attention is paid, in the left realist literature, to the enormous explosion of fraud and corruption that has accompanied the construction of a free market economy since 1979, and which has escalated since the Big Bang of 27 October 1986, when the London Stock Exchange was significantly opened up to a largely unregulated and competitive system for the marketing of financial securities of all kinds. There seems to be no interest either in the implications for the ordinary citizens of Britain of the Financial Services Act of 1986, which (*inter alia*) allows, for the first time in Britain, the direct and uncontrolled sale of financial services (like insurance) to customers on the basis of doorstep canvassing. We do not have the space here to offer a detailed empirical account of the enormity and frequency of the frauds (for example, involving 'insider-trades' and other manipulations of a deregulated market) which have already been uncovered in the wake of these major transformations (cf. Levi, 1987).

But we do strongly want to make the theoretical and sociological point that *the* fundamental transformation in Britain has been the construction of a 'free market economy' in the place of the exhausted Keynesian welfare state over which the last Labour government presided, and that this fundamental, structural transformation accentuates and even newly constructs some of the sense of despair and aggravation that characterizes certain parts of urban Britain. It is surely also the case that the emergence of the free market economy is the originating source of the emergence in Britain of the anti-social, parasitical weekend violence exhibited by some sections of the newly-monied classes in suburban or rural parts of the Home Counties, discussed by the Home Secretary himself but without reference to any account of the social conditions which produced such anti-social behaviour on the part of the sections of the 'respectable class'.

These are connections which *have* been made by the current Deputy Leader of the Labour Party, Roy Hattersley, albeit that Mr Hattersley is not widely known for his espousal of any radical alternative to the 'capitalist' economy itself. But they are not connections which are made apparent by left realists. One consequence, as we will try to show in our final set of comments, is that left realists seem unable to qualify their cautiously optimistic, realistic prescriptions about the potential of democratic policing and crime prevention schemes via any analysis of the overall dislocations wrought on the lives of communities or individuals by the general unleashing of market forces.[4] To make the point more directly, it is as if the left realists view the demoralization and fragmentation of working-class communities – and of social order in general – as resulting only from the marginalization of an underclass population of youth born of the rise of high technology and its impact on the labour market. There seems to be little interest among left realists in trying to make sense of the vast range of fundamental social, economic or, indeed, cultural consequences that have accompanied the emergence of a free market economy in Britain. So there is no detailed accounting, as we have said, of the insecurities and anxieties that now characterize even the employed population within the highly competitive and individualistic, non-unionized labour markets in Britain. And there is very little attention paid, either, to the cultural effects on the individual or group psyche of the steady advance, in British mass media and popular culture, of 'postmodernism', and even to the thesis – which social democrats ought surely to find of interest – that such a postmodern cultural field represents the *exhaustion*, rather than the self-confident advance, of a bourgeois politics (cf. Jameson, 1984). The possibility that is thereby suggested – for developing a moral and social critique of the whole direction of a free market society – is not even glimpsed. And the opportunity that this also presents – of developing the moral and philosophical context within which a struggle against the social disorder, violent crime (of 'morally brutalized youth') and economic frauds and corruptions of the newly-monied population starts to make *overall* sense – is lost. The moral and philosophical ground is thereby conceded to the new moral theorists of the right.

Left realism and the state

We have been suggesting that left realist criminology lacks a dynamic, complex and persuasive theory of the overall transformations that are currently occurring at the level of 'the economic', and that this has fundamental implications for the practical, realistic reforms which left realists want to advance as measures for the reduction of crime and the restoration of social order. It also has to be said that there are serious issues with respect to the left realists' implicit theory of that other classic object-of-analysis in the socialist and social-democratic tradition: the state.

It seems fair to say that the most obvious characteristics of the left realist 'theory' of the state is that it is largely a negation or denial of other existing left theories. It is, most obviously of all, a denial of the 'theory' of the state implicit in what the realists call left idealist criminology – in interactionism, in labelling theory and even, they imply, in the New Criminology. That is to say, the left realists reject any notion of a monolithic apparatus of social control, like Edwin Lemert's 'social control culture' or Howard Becker's 'zookeepers', existing outside and above civil society, but frequently imposed on individuals independently of any popular demand or need. They also firmly distance themselves from Leninist and other orthodox Marxist characterizations of the state as 'the night watchman of the bourgeoisie'; and seem drawn, instead, towards some form of revisionist and/or reformist conception of the state:

We reject the notion of conventional criminology that the state is a neutral

> institution acting in the universal interests of the population against, in this instance, the 'crime problem'. At the present moment, the British state represents very largely ruling-class interests, but gains can be wrung from it; reforms, however difficult, are possible and, in fact, relate to the State as in essence a site of contradicting interests. (Lea and Young, 1984: 103)

The question of how far reforms are possible (for instance in respect of introducing the democratic and/or accountable systems of policing outlined in the final chapter of Kinsey et al. (1986)) is not a question that can be settled in advance: that is a practical issue resolved on the terrains of policy construction, enactment and enforcement.

One effect of the adoption of this approach to the state in left criminological literature is that effective discussion of the state in contemporary Britain comes to be articulated in terms of an empirical and practical policy-oriented discussion of the criminal justice system (CJS) treated as a terrain that is more or less autonomous of the routine operation of other state functions, or indeed, of the logics of underlying free market economy itself. According the CJS this degree of autonomy does, of course, allow the left realists to advance reformative arguments with respect to the best, most desirable forms of operation of the system, but it also exempts the left realists from the responsibility of theorizing whether these reforms are likely or possible – given the existing forms and structures of the state in Britain, or indeed, in the light of the observable social effects and dislocations of the advance of a free market in labour.

This is not intended as a plea for the resurrection of structuralist theories of the state. It is not at all clear what any such theoreticism could contribute to our present difficulties. The left realists correctly insist that the *immediate* and *pressing* question is: what, practically speaking, is to be done? But it is not clear that this is a question which is entirely innocent with respect to a theory, of some order, of the role of the state in a free market economy.

In practical terms, the left realists appear to be arguing, as we have tried to show throughout this chapter, that a key social democratic project in the late 1980s is to take 'real' crime seriously and to advocate programmes for the improvement of policing and crime prevention programmes, based on democratic consultations but also constructed in recognition of the professional expertise of police. But they also *are* clearly concerned to differentiate their own realism from the 'realistic' commitment of the radical right to policies of 'systematic incapacitation' of 'criminals' (and the whole gamut of repressive measures which have been reactivated, without any perceptible effect on crime rates, in the British penal system). The argument which is developed, initially in respect of policing in *Losing the Fight against Crime*, is for a 'minimalist' criminal justice system, which is capable of intervening firmly in circumstances of absolute necessity but which also uses the most minimal amount of force and coercion required:

> The philosophy of minimalism (including minimal policing)...demarcat(es) the minimal, if necessary intervention of the coercive powers of the State. Minimalism, in its continued commitment to a reformed, if greatly diminished criminal justice system, differs, of course, from abolition. It also differs from the minimization of state intervention advocated by American liberals such as Norval Morris, or the radical non-interventionism of deviancy theorists such as Edwin Schur. (Young, 1987: 353)

The commitment of a minimalist criminal justice system, the argument continues, is to 'the minimum intervention necessary to protect the population against predatory criminal forces . . . and unallayed market forces' (Young, 1987: 353).

The residual and symptomatic mention here of market forces inadvertently directs attention to one of key consequences of the left realists' treatment of the CJS as a more or less autonomous terrain, and their failure to give consideration to the classic question of the relationship of the state and the economy. The transformation of the British economy over the last 12 years has *not*, of course, involved any *overall* rolling-back of 'the state' from the exercise of direction over the economy nor, indeed, from the exercise of a directive influence over civil society as a whole. But there *has* simultaneously been a marked withdrawal of the state from a vast range of activities (and expenditures) in respect of health, education, welfare, urban transportation, public housing and planning – in respect, in short, of *public provision.* One of the unmistakable features of British society in the late 1980s is, indeed, the absolute impoverishment (the under-financing and generalized neglect) of public spaces (in transport systems, in hospitals, schools, etc). This crisis of public provision and public space continually threatens to break through, and to contradict, the otherwise unchallenged hegemony of free market thinking in contemporary Britain. It found expression, in particular, in the public debates that occurred in the aftermath of a range of disasters occurring during 1985 to 1989, which seemed increasingly to be connected in the public mind (the fires at the Bradford City soccer stadium in June 1985 [55 dead] and at Manchester Airport, the sinking of the British-owned ferry *The Herald of Free Enterprise* in Zeebrugge Harbour, most poignantly of all for many Londoners, the death by fire of 31 passengers at King's Cross Underground Station in November 1987, and in April 1989 the 95 deaths at Hillsborough (cf. Taylor, 1990a)). Less dramatically but equally insistently, public concern about vandalism and litter, and their effects on the environment as well as their potential in respect of public safety, has been growing exponentially. In the area of litter management, in particular, pressure groups have been increasingly making the vital connection between the withdrawal of the state from certain public expenditure functions (local authority provision) and the perceptible growth of a sense, among citizens in general, that literally no one has responsibility for custodianship of public space.

The importance of this crisis in public provision for social democrats is unmistakable. For left realist criminologists, in particular, there is the opportunity of being able to offer an amount of *the genesis of the conditions of public neglect* which, with right realists like James Q. Wilson, the left realists see to be independently contributory to community demoralization and crime: the powerful and distinctive point being, however, that such an account could powerfully be linked to an argument about the responsibilities of the state in respect of public, collective provision (especially in areas, like the downtown core, where voluntary endeavour is clearly not about to emerge on a 24-hour basis). The point is to make connections at the level of political and policy discourse between the different *social consequences* of 'free market' government and the departure of the state from key areas of public provision. The realist element in this resides in the recognition of a developing popular anxiety over the tangible crisis of public space; the social democratic element resides in the generalization to a viable political conclusion, a persuasive articulation of the positive role of the state in the provision of a public good. The potential in this for a critique of the forms of public service provided by *the market*, restricted as this is almost by definition to provision of comfort and security only at the point of consumption, should be obvious.

To argue in this way is not to try to 'reinvent the wheel' of a cumbersome, centralized and bureaucratic form of statist social democracy. But it is to try and articulate a form of political discourse which connects state activity and provision with some idea of the public good. The opportunities to do this, in a free market economy like that which is being elaborated in Britain, present themselves constantly across a broad range of areas (like the question of public health and state education). But it is not clear that this project of mobilization of the state as a public good is best thought of as a generalization out from the left realists' discussion of the need for a *minimalist* criminal justice system.

Confronted as they were (at the end of the nineteenth century and the beginnings of the twentieth) by the growth of business, finance capital and commerce, utopian social democratic thinkers like Edward Carpenter and John Ruskin felt impelled to try and draw up a moral and aesthetic vision of alternative forms of economic and social organization attuned to social need. They also felt impelled to challenge the moral and philosophical foundations of the various forms of utilitarian 'political economy' which celebrated the free play of the market forces. These utopian visions have never been concretely realized, but, as Zygmunt Bauman (1976) and others have trenchantly observed, they have remained important influences in even the most realist of social democratic policy thinking. They have also been important and influential at particular historical moments, in mobilizing the mass of the citizens electorally or in giving encouragement to political and social movements or individuals working towards the achievement of specific, reformist goals. It is not simply starry-eyed to make reference, here, to the enormous, independent influence of a radical, utopian vision, born of the experience of the 1930s recession and the struggles against Fascism, in the construction of the agenda of Social Reconstruction of the post-war Labour government, and pursued with a real commitment and some realistic, strategic sense between 1945 and 1948. It was a vision which was concerned to rehouse the people, to provide for their health *and* to provide for equality of educational opportunity; and these were all objectives which were *substantially* achieved through political activity within and through the state.

If there is one important lesson *for social democrats* in opposition to learn from the Thatcher years, it is that the state is in a particular important sense 'pluralist' and 'autonomous' of capital: it is that the state is a 'space' on which very considerable political advances can be made, especially by a committed political party, under a leadership which is capable of strategic shifts in the realist project of maintaining public and popular support for a utopian project of social reconstruction. It is not clear, however, how a *social democratic sense of utopian possibility* is realizable through the left realists' accommodation, in respect of the operation of the criminal justice system, to a minimalist state. Moreover, since it is not really clear what kind of ultimate vision of social order lies behind the calls for democratic policing and community crime prevention, then the left realists are prey, like the Labour Party itself, to the accusation that it 'has no moral agenda of its own except an inherited conservative one' (Hall, 1988: 27). As with the Labour Party itself, then, it is difficult to see left realism, at least in its earliest formulations, as 'a force that is actively shaping the culture, shaping desire' (Hall, 1988: 27).

The emphases in left realist writing have, however, undergone a considerable change since 1981–2. In earlier years, the uniform sense of despair which accompanied the first two years of the Thatcher government, with a doubling of unemployment and the outbreak of violent and quite unprecedented inner-city riots, very much focused the minds of many social democratic thinkers on the development of popular policies in key areas of public concern, with the aim in view of a victory against 'Thatcherism' at the first available electoral opportunity. Nearly 12 years on from 1979, it is not clear that the Conservative Party's moral and political hegemony is under threat from even the most 'moderate' or 'realist' of Labour Party leaderships, even if there was a possibility of a Labour electoral victory. There *is* a sense, in 1991 that left realists, like all other social democratic thinkers in Britain, have begun to work through a much more fundamental moral and philosophical alternative to life in a free market society: a recent Fabian pamphlet, jointly authored by some of the left realist school, speaks urgently and eloquently of its 'core idea' being 'the reconstruction of a civic culture ... founded securely on citizens' rights and obligations' (Corrigan et al., 1988: 16). This is a welcome development in the left realist position. 'Social democracy' in general is in need not just of a recognition of the pluralism in civil society and the reformability of the state (both of which visions *are* obscured in the *orthodox* class analysis and state theory). There is an urgent need also for the self-confident assertion of a *moral* politics prioritizing the public good and public, collective provision. In our own field of endeavour – the study of 'crime' – there is a need for a clear recognition that the generalized condition of disorder in Britain is fundamentally a social and political phenomenon, to which there are public rather than market solutions. If this, properly speaking, is a 'utopian' rather than a 'realist' position, then so also, in 1979, arguing the alternative case but taking seriously the real obstacles in *its* path, was Thatcherism itself.

Notes

This chapter is a revised version of a paper first presented to the American Society of Criminology meetings, Chicago, November 1988.

1. Final speeches of 'Eddie' and 'Carol' in *Road*, by Jim Cartwright, first performed at the Royal Court Theatre Upstairs, London, 22 March 1986.

2. I am aware of some criminological writing of a left realist character in the USA, most notably by Bertram Gross (1982), Ray Michalowski (1983) and Peter Iadicola (1986), but it seems fair to say that these individual interventions have not given rise, for whatever reason, to a recognized 'school' of American left realist criminology, or to a series of books and papers acting as a resource for such a strategic perspective in a broader 'left' or democratic constituency.

3. One of the sub-themes in this chapter, indeed, is that the emphasis which was placed on 'law and order' by the first two Thatcher administrations has now been elided, strategically and to great effect, into a more generalized campaign for the 'remoralization' of British society. This campaign extends from coercive interventions (involving censorship and other statutory controls) into popular television and video, to the wholesale reorganization of state education (articulated, in part, around rhetorics of moral order and 'standards'). I discuss this shift in the strategic rhetorics and legislative initiatives of the Thatcher government in Taylor (1987). The emergence of this new

emphasis on individual moral responsibility poses quite a different challenge to social democratic opponents than the earlier Conservative preoccupation with the imposition and/or intensification of penal discipline.

    4. For a series of essays on the social dislocations resulting from this unleashing of market forces in five different societies, see Taylor (1990b).

References

BBC (1961) *A Report on Some Audience Research Enquiries Connected with the Television Series 'Crime'*. VR/61/1 (Mimeo, 89 pp.).

Bauman, Zygmunt (1976) *Socialism: The Active Utopia*. London: George Allen & Unwin.

Boseley, Sarah (1987) 'Foreign bodies', *The Guardian*, 18 November.

Bradley, Ian (1988) 'Freedom to be a nuisance', *The Guardian*, 11 June.

Bridges, Lee and Gilroy, Paul (1982) 'Striking back', *Marxism Today*, 26(6): 34–5.

Carpenter, Edward (1905) *Prisons, Police and Punishment*. London: Arthur C. Fifield.

Cartwright, Jim (1986) *Road*. London: Methuen Paperback Original.

Christoph, James B. (1962) *Capital Punishment and British Politics*. London: George Allen & Unwin.

Cohen, Stan (1986) 'Community control: to demystify or to reaffirm?' in H. Bianchi and R. van Swaaningen (eds), *Abolitionism: Towards a Non-repressive Approach to Crime*. Amsterdam: Free University Press.

Corrigan, Paul, Jones, Trevor, Lloyd, John and Young, Jock (1988) *Socialism, Merit and Efficiency*. Fabian Society Pamphlet No. 530. London: The Fabian Society.

Dahrendorf, Ralf (1985) *Law and Order* (The Hamlyn Lectures, Thirty-Seventh Series). London: Stevens.

Department of Education and Science (1987) *Education Reform: the Government's Proposals for Schools*. London: HMSO (Central Office of Information).

Gilroy, Paul (1982) 'The myth of black criminality', in R. Miliband and J. Saville (eds), *Socialist Register 1982*. London: Merlin Press.

Gilroy, Paul and Sim, Joe (1985) 'Law and order: the state of the left', *Capital and Class* (revised version in P. Scraton (ed.), *Law, Order and the Authoritarian State*. Milton Keynes: Open University Press, 1987).

Gorz, André (1982) *Farewell to the Working Class*, London: Pluto Press.

Gross, Bertram (1982) 'Some anti-crime strategies for progressives', *Crime and Social Justice*, 17: 51–4.

Hall, Stuart (1988) 'Thatcher's lessons', *Marxism Today*, March: 20–27.

Hulsman, Louk (1986) 'Critical criminology and the concept of crime', *Contemporary Crises* 10(1): 63–80.

Hurd, Douglas (1988a) 'Douglas Hurd's Tamworth Manifesto', *London Review of Books*, 17 March: 7.

Hurd, Douglas (1988b) 'Citizenship in the Tory democracy', *New Statesman*, 29 April: 14.

Hurd, Douglas, (1988c) 'Hurd wants "civic responsibility" taught in schools', *The Independent*, 12 July.

Iadicola, Peter (1986) 'Community crime control strategies', *Crime and Social Justice*, 25: 140–65.

Jameson, Frederic (1984) 'Postmodernism, or the cultural logic of late capitalism', *New Left Review*, 146, July–August.

Jones, Trevor, MacLean, Brian and Young, Jock (1986) *The Islington Crime Survey*. Aldershot: Gower Press.

Kinsey, Richard, Lea, John and Young, Jock (1986) *Losing the Fight against Crime*. Oxford: Blackwell.

Laclau, Ernesto and Mouffe, Chantal (1985) *Hegemony and Socialist Strategy*. London: Verso.

Lea, John and Young, Jock (1984) *What is to be Done about Law and Order?* Harmondsworth: Penguin (in conjunction with the Socialist Society).

Leadbeater, Charles (1987) *The Politics of Prosperity*. London: Fabian Society Pamphlet No. 523.

Levi, Michael (1987) *Regulating Fraud: White Collar Crime and the Criminal Process*. London: Tavistock.

MacLeod, Mary and Saraga, Esther (1988) 'Against orthodoxy', *New Statesman/ Society*, 1 July: 15–19.

Matthews, Roger (1987) 'Taking realist criminology seriously', *Contemporary Crises*, 11(4): 371–402.

Matthews, Roger and Young, Jock (eds) (1986) *Confronting Crime*. London: Sage.

Matthews, Roger and Young, Jock (eds) (1992) *Issues in Realist Criminology*. London: Sage.

Michalowski, Ray (1983) 'Crime control in the 1980s: a progressive agenda', *Crime and Social Justice*, 19: 13–22.

Parker, Howard J. (1988) *Living with Heroin: the Impact of a Drugs Epidemic on an English Community*. Milton Keynes: Open University Press.

Pearson, Geoffrey (1988) *The New Heroin Users*. Oxford: Blackwell.

Poggi, Gianfranco (1978) *The Development of the Modern State*. London: Hutchinson.

Scraton, Phil (ed) (1987) *Law, Order and the Authoritarian State*. Milton Keynes: Open University Press.

Seabrook, Jeremy (1987) 'The horror of Hungerford', *New Society*, 28 August: 15–16.

Steinert, Heinz (1985) 'The amazing new left law and order campaign: some thoughts on anti-utopianism and possible futures', *Contemporary Crises*, 9(4): 327–34.

Taylor, Ian (1987) 'Law and order, moral order: the changing rhetorics of the Thatcher government', in R. Miliband, L. Panitch and J. Saville (eds), *The Socialist Register 1987*. London: Merlin Press.

Taylor, Ian (1990a) 'Hillsborough, 15 April 1989', *New Left Review*, 177: 87–110.

Taylor, Ian (ed.) (1990b) *The Social Effects of Free Market Policies: An International Text*. Hemel Hempstead: Harvester Wheatsheaf.

Thatcher, Margaret (1988) *Address to the General Assembly of the Church of Scotland*. 21 May.

Wilson, J.Q. and Kelling, G.L. (1982) 'The police and neighbourhood safety: broken windows', *Atlantic Monthly*, 127: 28–38.

Young, Jock (1987) 'The tasks facing a realist criminology', *Contemporary Crises*, 11(4): 337–56.

Young, Jock (1988) 'Radical criminology in Britain: the emergence of a competing paradigm', *British Journal of Criminology*, 28(2): 289–313.

5 Realist criminology: a critique

Vincenzo Ruggiero

In his 'vocabulary of culture and society' Raymond Williams devotes several pages to the key word 'realism', stressing that this word polemically advocates the concrete against the abstract, materialism versus idealism. Realism implies on the one hand the 'impatience of one sense of practical' and on the other a 'tone of limited calculation' typical of politicians and businessmen. The sense of practical and limited calculation can conjure up evocations of reality merely through its appearance and reduce the analysis to surface observation: realism can then become prosaic and be accused of evading the real (Williams, 1976). I will try to examine to what extent realist criminology exposes itself to these dangers, while locating its assumptions and practices within the general developments of current criminology.

The emergence of realism

Frequently the existence of an academic discipline evolves irrespective of the evolution of the social phenomena to which it is directed. As regards criminology, we are witnessing a process of *politicization*. This is a function of changing political imperatives and the attempts to create a one-dimensional society aimed at constraining critical discourses. The process of politicization is also favoured by those criminologists who feel committed to the cause of 'serving' the community. A salvational and protective function has in fact been adopted both by mainstream scholars and so-called 'radical criminologists'. The latter still identify themselves with the leading edge of social struggles and see themselves as 'organic intellectuals'. Thus the old allegiances are salvaged despite a drastic shift of terrain. Some radical criminologists now act not so much for the marginalized and the expelled but only for those subjects who inhabit the legitimate political arena. The notion of avant garde is translated into that of expert. The point of reference is removed from civil society and relocated in party political discourse. In this context intellectuals become less engaged with social movements on the ground and more concerned with electoral achievements. In the process of pursuing these new parliamentary objectives there is always the danger of losing touch with everyday needs and aspirations and, in the words of Baudrillard, society becomes degraded, mortified and moralized (Baudrillard, 1978).

Through politicization, criminology becomes more concerned with the forms of representation than with the events themselves. In other words, events and conflicts are selected and focused upon not on the basis of their social or criminological relevance, but on the basis of their potential for political and electoral advantage. It has to be added that the reproduction of the political language follows its own internal logic and, paradoxically, may even lose its connection to the social forces it claims to represent (Tronti, 1976; Cacciari, 1978). Criminology can become as 'autonomous' as the political apparatus in which it is entangled: it may give the impression of responding to problematic situations and tackling social crises, but it may in fact be managing its own crises. So criminology, even in its radical variants, may become less concerned with crime than with its own reproduction.

Within this process of politicization, criminologists are under growing pressure to produce immediate tangible results. And as a consequence criminology has become increasingly policy oriented. In this process there is a tendency for conceptual and theoretical works to be discarded or regarded as indulgent. Because they are not measurable or immediately applicable, they are denied the validity that 'scientific' or 'concrete' criminological studies are awarded. This process does not involve a contraction of the subject nor a reduction in the number of professionals operating in the field. On the contrary, the number of researchers and experts continues to grow.

A related trend involves the movement towards administrativization. This movement has already been characterized as a shift in the treatment of subjects whereby 'the presupposition and concern is neither an organic human community nor an atomic individual: the presupposition and concern is a non-human abstracted ruling interest, public policy or ongoing activity, of which human beings are subordinates, functionaries, or carriers' (Kamenka and Tay, 1975: 138). The emphasis is less upon the causes of crime than the managerial measures which can be employed to tackle it. The preoccupation is increasingly with inputs and outputs and less with the pursuit of justice. The point of decision making tends to shift from the criminal justice arena to the often less visible bureaucratic authorities.

The emphasis upon administrative modes of intervention stands in contrast to another current tendency which claims to reduce the level of bureaucratic inefficiency with more commercialized and privatized approaches. We have seen the creation of a new criminological market where prevention and incapacitation are sold in a growing climate of competition. Crime ends up by producing entrepreneurial opportunities, the aim being not that of reducing it, but that of making it more productive (Ryan and Ward, 1989). The difficulties in assessing the quality of the product sold (prevention, incapacitation and punishment) does not stop the commercial contest. What seems to count in this market is the ability to present an attractive product. Well advertised national and international conferences, press coverage and official endorsements, may all boost the market share of the different criminological firms, but the outcome of their respective products is rarely subject to proper verification.

Commensurate with this tendency is the exclusive priority assigned to *quantitative* as opposed to *qualitative* research. The former approach is consistent with policy performances and supposedly permits evaluations in the adequacy of projects. The qualitative approach, in turn, presupposes a greater amount of 'sociological imagination' than is currently required. Imaginative ideas are discouraged, and data gathering is regarded as the ideal substitute for theory: *sociology finally turns into accountancy.* Moreover, the quantitative obsession *objectifies* the 'problematic situations', thus allowing the reintroduction of certain positivistic notions which were previously rejected.

Left realist criminology is both a product of and a reaction to these tendencies. The left realists have tried to sidestep the bifurcation of administrative criminology and radical criminology and to overcome the impasse (Young, 1988a). By doing so they have attempted to recapture the issue of law and order. Taking distance from the right realists, with whom they share a 'commitment to taking crime seriously', they claim that they 'critically explore the complex reality of crime as it is experienced in everyday life' (Matthews, 1987). On the other hand, their criticism takes issue with official administrative criminology for its assumptions that the causes of crime are either relatively unimportant or politically impossible to tackle. They have also opposed the 'romantic image of the criminal portrayed in radical criminology', which has gone very close to denying the existence of crime itself.

The critique of radical criminology

One of the merits ascribed to the realists is the attempt to reorient attention from the institutional processes of criminalization towards 'problematic situations' as they arise and are perceived in the social arena. This shift initially heralded an important innovation. Large sectors of critical criminology have in fact focused on reactions to crime, on social constructions of images of deviance, on the artificial creation of anti-social behaviours, and have ended up by frequently neglecting those social phenomena which are conventionally called criminal. The rejection of the official definitions has extended to a refusal to interpret the material acts which underlie the official definitions themselves. The fear of fuelling moral panic has led a large number of critical criminologists to regard those acts as mere reflections of formal intervention. Critical criminology did indeed become increasingly vague in its choice of subjects of study. It was reflecting on a reflection: it focused upon diverse visions and images, the initial sources of which were slowly vanishing (Kinsey et al., 1986).

In its more inspired moments critical criminology provided a useful excursion into the field of social constructionism, as when, for example, it indicated how certain behaviours can become criminalized through a process of social definition and negotiation. At its best, critical criminology conferred a notion of historical and social relativity to 'crime' by questioning its presumed essentialist nature. At its worst, critical criminology was in danger of evolving into pure political propaganda. It spoke on behalf of 'criminalized' individuals who had probably never dreamt of appointing criminologists as their ideological representatives. Critical criminology adopted a pedagogical model and claimed to represent the underdog and the underworld. However, its anti-correctionalism provided a disincentive to analyse this very underworld in any detail (Baratta, 1982).

It can hardly be denied that, in this context, the impact of realist criminology, although it may be associated with national developments in Britain, initially also had an international relevance. In Italy for example, when the realist perspective started circulating, a sense of disorientation emerged. This was due both to the political shift of former radical criminologists and to the realization of a lacuna in the existing paradigms. It has to be noted that the Italian judicial culture has in recent years been fed by a series of *emergencies*: so-called terrorism, organized crime and drugs. These 'permanent emergencies' have deeply transformed the judicial system along with the common perception of illegal behaviours. Now, if we seek information, descriptions and interpretations of the *internal economy* (both ideological and material) of the above mentioned phenomena, we have to be content with information concerning the social images and institutional reactions to them. Regarded as slippery arenas where moral panics could easily thrive, terrorism, organized crime and drugs are rarely deemed worth investigating or understanding.

In sum, the left realist proposals performed the role of pointing at the polarization of the field of study in criminology while denouncing a paradoxical 'disappearance' of the objects of its study. They highlighted the need for less symbolically oriented discourses and more structurally oriented analysis: the need to observe the roots of those problematic situations which permit *disciplinary symbols* and fears to grow and prosper. The left realist project sounded very challenging, but it is not clear how its initial promises were fulfilled.

Which victims?

In a geometrical representation of crime, the left realists have suggested an ideal *square* whose vertices are occupied respectively by the victim, the offender, the state and the public. This square represents the framework in which the social and institutional actors create and define crime. How is the first vertex analysed?

The realists express a general enthusiasm for victimization research because it partly discloses the dark figure of crime and shifts the focus away from what are traditionally police priorities to those which are the priorities of the wider public (Young, 1988b). Aggregate data, we are told, does not account for the real predicaments of people: it describes crime as a rare occurrence and the average chance of being victimized as extremely low. Locally centred research proves instead that the risk of being assaulted and burgled, for instance, can be in certain areas several times higher than average risk. A realistic depiction of crime points out its specific geography: crime is localized, it is not evenly distributed and affects certain categories of people, usually the more vulnerable, more seriously than others. It is added that more vulnerable victims are less likely to report crime because they are both less 'credible' and are themselves less confident of the institutions appointed to resolve their problems as victims. A realist approach also considers the qualitative aspects of crime in that it highlights the unwillingness of vulnerable people to report crimes committed within their family, and their propensity to report crimes against personal property rather than crimes of violence (Kinsey et al., 1986).

A different picture of 'problematic situations' is presented in which the day-to-day experiences of people are attributed a crucial role in describing the real dimension of offences and their impact. The accumulation of apparently trivial offences, incivilities, sexual and racial harassment portrays a situation where, contrary to the reassuring aggregate data, people's lives can be made a misery. Defying the official 'objective' definitions, the realists suggest that more attention should be paid to the subjective perceptions of the various subgroups in society and to their respective problems as they arise and are perceived in their specific arenas. In an indisputable indictment of official victimization research, the realists proclaim that it commonly trivializes that which is important and makes important that which is trivial (Young, 1988b).

The critique of the official victimization studies put forward by the realists is, however, not complete. To be consistent, they would need to develop a version of this critique against their own victimization surveys. More wary authors have in fact pointed out that the reorientation of criminology towards the victim offers an exhausted discipline the opportunity to revitalize itself and restore 'political' legitimacy. In a scenario dominated by 'penological pessimism', many prefer to operate in a safer terrain, that of the victim, which requires neither the exaltation nor the stigmatization of the offender. Victimology may be seen as acting as a 'safety belt' for criminology by boosting its role and retrieving its identity. Controversies are defused, differences in schools of thought are flattened: criminology is given back an artificial cohesion and renewed momentum. The benefits of this unity cannot be measured in terms of immediate results, but are linked to the enhanced status of criminology as an academic discipline and the status of its representatives as criminologists – irrespective of the internal paradigmatic differences (Fattah, 1986; Mawby and Gill, 1987; Wright and Galaway, 1989).

The terrain of the victims, moreover, offers itself as a particularly attractive issue for the politicians, who can readily express their desire to tackle crime and to improve the quality of life of citizens and voters. Who would not support those who defend the victims of crime? In a period of aetiological crisis, of professional and political uncertainty, victimology offers a useful shift of focus and a new field of study.

There are reasons to doubt that, even in locally centred research, the answers given by individual respondents constitute the reality of crime; and that the addition of individual opinions, expressed in merely private contexts, produces what we term as 'public opinion'. In fact, the responses of the public are not independent from the interaction with the criminologists who carry out the surveys and from the artificial situation created by them. Little attention is devoted by the realists to the effects of their own presence in the field and how their very work affects the evaluations and definitions of crime. It is well known, for example, that when sensitizing the public through preventive campaigns, unintended effects may easily result. These vary between 'undesirable reactions to crime, high emotional involvement or a high risk-assessment' (Winkel, 1987).

Ten years ago, in more sophisticated analyses, certain realists stressed the double, opaque and contradictory structure of reality, and it is legitimate to wonder why the same opacity is not attributed by them to the reality as presented in their own victimization surveys (Cohen and Young, 1981).

If we examine situations in more detail, other notions of victim and other aspects of victimization emerge which are lacking in the realist approach. The first aspect deserving more attention is linked to the fact that the victims of crime are not always more vulnerable than offenders. Specific studies need to focus on the power relationship underlying each single act and each problematic situation. In a complete typology of criminal acts, those behaviours should be considered which, through economic appropriation or even through the exercise of ritual non-serious violence, aim at the 'socialization' of those who perform them. It would be naive to regard these acts, especially those economically motivated, as exemplary bids to redistribute wealth. When the offender is socially more vulnerable, predatory behaviours may at most have an educational function, in that they allow the temporary reversal of power relations. Some crimes confirm the existing distribution of power, but some do not. It is not enough for criminologists to assume the relations of dominance in victim–offender relations nor simply to present themselves as defenders of the weak. Their task is to uncover and explain the complex processes through which 'victims' and 'offenders' are reproduced.

It should be noted that, in a sense, victims can become double victims in that they can become victims of victimology itself. That is they can be victimized by the stereotypes imposed upon them. These stereotypes relate to their alleged incapacity to defend themselves. They also relate to the incapacity for victims to define themselves as such, the condition of victim being constructed externally and despite them. Subsequently, the victims of victimology are regarded and treated as objects of tutelage, as 'judicial goods' who are required not to 'interfere' in the situations in which they are actors. They are requested to entrust their inviolability to external agencies which are normally structured to reproduce principles of dependency and delegation rather than principles of autonomy (Christie, 1982).

Other types of victimization can occur through the mobilization of institutional fear. This is to be analysed in the context of the official fear of crowds, mass assemblies of people, contemporary mobs which recall analogous terror aroused by urban gatherings in previous centuries. Examples of victims of institutional fear can be found among football supporters and those attending street festivals. It has been argued that these types of victims can also be found among the soaring prison population. Steven Box (1987), for instance, has suggested that in periods of recession, institutional fear subscribes to the belief that unemployment causes crime, and this in turn results in stricter practices of control and punishment.

A final notion of victimization can be added to the list. There are 'invisible victims'. That is, those who are not directly aware of their victimization. For example those victimized by pollution, unemployment, inadequate services, exploitation and dangerous goods. Curiously enough, in these cases, the offenders often express more concern about crime in general than their victims (see Pearce and Tombs, 1992).

Drug abuse: the realist argument

As stressed before, the square of crime suggested by the realists constitutes a very promising analytical device, in that it contextualizes different actors simultaneously and points at their interactions in the social production of what we call crime. The realists, though, have not so far analysed thoroughly the four vertices of the square (see Lea, Chapter 3). The above brief discussion was meant to hint at the flaws in their approach to the victims of crime. Let's now move to the other vertex: the offenders.

One problem the realists have become aware of is the need for a political economy of crime (see Taylor, Chapter 4). I suggest that this may focus on the terrain of the labour market and explain the relationships between unemployment, recession and crime. On the other hand, I believe that a political economy of crime may be centred on the 'criminal labour market' and explain the internal dynamics of it. In accepting this distinction a notion of crime ought to be implied whereby crime itself is regarded as an enterprise, with its own invest-ment choices, its own production, its own living labour and reserve army. There are obviously areas of overlap between the labour market and the 'criminal labour market'. But this cannot exempt us from analysing the internal dynamics of the specific economy of crime, its internal relationships and its evolution.

When trying to come to terms with the political economy of crime, one of the terrains which ideally lends itself to scrutiny is that of illicit drug use and distribution. The left realists have attempted to do so in a recent contribution (Young, 1988c). Interestingly, one of the first critical studies on drugs conducted in Britain was by Jock Young, who is now a leading realist. He underlined how the intervention of the official agencies adds to the marginalization of the drug users, thus making them more inclined to use drugs (Young, 1971). This assump-tion was consistent with critical criminological paradigms: problematic use of drugs and addiction only arise when the official agencies intervene and create images of deviance, socially recognizable prob-lems which otherwise would not be considered to be problems. Drug users end up facing a so-called cognitive dissonance, which they resolve by conforming to the image imposed on them, and not only become addicts but also adopt all those social features artificially associated with addiction. The process of addiction, in other words, is explained through social rather than physical dynamics. It is the result of labelling.

In a more recent essay, some attempt has been made to add a realist dimension to this analysis. Strangely, however, we find a repetition of much of the previous 'idealist' analysis:

> The social reaction against drug use, despite the rhetoric and sometimes the reality of the humanitarianism it expresses, achieves precisely the opposite of its manifest aims. Instead of liberating the individual from addiction it confirms him as a deviant rather than obviating suffering; it ensures that the misery becomes inescapable. The myth that illicit drug use is intrinsically unpleasurable is thereby made to come true, and justified as 'treatment'. (Young, 1988c: 446)

This argument seems to share a lot with the so-called non-interventionist perspective according to which the hedonistic use of both cannabis and opiates is made illegal solely because some substances are selected and demonized.

The realist approach seems limited to a statement of principle when it is stressed that: 'there *is* a problem of drug use within society, but the real problem is caricatured, exaggerated and converted into a moral panic by powerful forces in our society. The mass media take real fears about drugs and inject hysteria into people's mind' (Young, 1988c: 449). This is a weak and hardly original statement. The difference between a realist analysis and that of 'idealists' is far from clear. There is also a problem in relation to intervention which arises from this approach. It is suggested that we have to eliminate the underlying causes, look for viable alternatives to the use of drugs, avoid the onset of deviancy amplification, and change the social situation of the addicts. These recommendations do not distinguish a 'realist' approach from other approaches.

In hinting at the solution to the drug problem, intervention at street level is also advocated. William Burroughs is called in support of this view: 'If we wish to annihilate the junk pyramid, we must start with the bottom of the pyramid, the addict in the street.' We can assume that this resolution is shared by the realists in that it is commensurate with their emphasis on street crime, working-class victimization, incivilities and disturbances which *realistically* produce hardship in daily life (Jones et al., 1986; Painter et al., 1989). This resolution has been reiterated more recently, when, in their suggestions for tailoring police work to the nature of specific crimes, the left realists have argued that: 'The trafficking of hard drugs must be combatted on every level from international supply to street level. Street level dealing is, however, the weakest point in the chain and must be tackled effectively with the proviso that sentences should not be disproportionate and unjust' (Crawford et al., 1990: 8.22).

While stressing the need to stop addiction at street level, the realists do not seem to realize that this is currently the favoured policy. This is because the street level drug user population is both inexperienced and vulnerable. Clumsy as they are, and most dangerous not only to others but to themselves, many beginners hold such limited professionalism that they are exposed to many hazards in their day-to-day activities. Like other workers in highly risky productive activities, they can hardly be simply regarded as offenders, but rather as products (and in a sense victims) of the criminal labour market into which they have been recruited.

One reason why the realists may have come to their conclusions is due to an effect of the statistics. Both in local and national victimization surveys the depiction of the drug problem is highly selective. In the latest *British Crime Survey* the term 'drug' is not even listed in the final, elaborate, glossary (Mayhew et al., 1989).

What is missing from the realist approach is an analysis of the operation of the market and how it creates different pressures and vulnerabilities. Such an analysis would indicate that the street level user is both an economic victim and is imminently replaceable. He or she may be the weakest link in the pyramid but because of the numbers involved it would take a massive degree of intervention for the pyramid to collapse. The other consequence of directing intervention principally at the low level street user is professionalization.

These points can be exemplified with examples from recent developments in Italy. The recent growth in immigration from North Africa has had visible repercussions in the *criminal labour market*. The newcomers are allured into street level dealing, whereas the more experienced, formerly small dealers, are slowly escalating the hierarchy of the criminal career. The immigrants are being employed in the riskiest operations of the drug economy, and as a consequence the prison population in Italy is becoming increasingly North African and desperate (and 'unskilled'). Simultaneous with the creation of a number of expendable minions servicing the market, there is a drive towards more structured and professionalized operations. These developments are not oppositional. On the contrary it is the employment of one which allows for the promotion of the other (Ruggiero, 1986).

The realists, with their emphasis on street crime, tend to neglect the fact that street crime itself is often encompassed in organized crime and that both, simultaneously, need to be described and analysed in their social and economic contexts. The drug economy involves an identifiable hierarchy of connected relations between different types of offences and offenders, with skilled and professional operators at the top and unskilled and disorganized individuals at the bottom. The realists, so far, have failed to appraise these connected relations (Ruggiero, 1989).

An incomplete aetiology

The failure of the left realists to examine corporate and organized crime, and to account for the relationship between the latter and street crime, suggests an obvious question. Are their tools of analysis adequate to explain both corporate and organized crime? Their aetiological view of crime in general needs to be examined in order to answer this question.

Lea and Young stress that crime is not a product of the individual separate from social structure, nor do they endorse the view of those who 'point to the paramount effect of structure bearing down upon the individual' (Lea and Young, 1984: 60). In their vision there is no space for 'organic' nor 'social' determinism. Their approach is a constructivist one, in the sense that in their 'square of crime' all vertices play a role, in a given historical and social context, in defining 'crime'.

As for more specific causes of crime, the realists rely very heavily upon the notion of relative deprivation, defined by them as the excess of expectations over opportunities. In their opinion, when this is linked with marginality, the discontent cannot be channelled into political forms. 'Instead, the most obvious solution is that of crime. Meanwhile communities breakdown facilitates crime by drastically undermining the process of social control' (Lea and Young, 1984: 263).

The left realists claim the definitions of crime to be complex and only contextually appraisable. But according to the critique put forward by de Leo, 'this complexity, rich and promising, evolves into something rigid and poor, when the authors define and use their two key concepts, discontent and relative deprivation, and regard them as *the causes* of crime and of any other form of antisocial behaviour' (de Leo, 1986: 461). In de Leo's opinion, the realists devote a lot of work to the explanation of processes such as 'discontent' and 'relative deprivation', but do not manage to explain the relationships between these processes and crime. 'We are left with the impression that discontent and relative deprivation mean tout-court predisposition to crime, in a very traditional sense' (de Leo, 1986: 464).

And moreover, how do discontent and relative deprivation explain corporate and organized crime? Their aetiology does not include notions of 'crime as work' or of criminal organizations as enterprises. Nor do they seem to take into account those theories which focus on the processes of learning, differential associations, and those theories which might allow us to go beyond the explanation of street crime (Sutherland, 1940).

Tamar Pitch also sees in the realist approach a simplification whereby the link between the contradictions of capitalism, crime, its definition and repression, consists of the explicative couple: relative deprivation–discontent (Pitch, 1986). She notes in this an endorsement of a Mertonian scheme of interpretation, where only the relationship between the contradictions of capitalism and a specific kind of crime can be explained. But again, how does anomie contribute to the analysis of organized and white-collar crime? Pitch concludes that the relationship between relative deprivation and discontent, and between discontent and crime 'is taken for granted, not unlike in the model of interpretation that the realists term as left idealism' (Pitch, 1986: 473).

It would be intriguing to evaluate how much 'idealism' is still left in the realist paradigm. Their search for a strong and central cause of crime parallels their anxiety to found a new school, and their feverish need to say something new. In some instances, in fact, the realist stance seems to denote itself viable because of a few enunciations of principle, or for mere semantic options. The use of keywords like 'idealism' and 'impossibilism' is sometimes the only signal that the author is a 'realist' (Matthews, 1988). Pitch terms this as a 'paradigmatic anxiety', and explains it as a reaction of the realists to the current social complexity which they refuse to handle. Their search for a strong and central cause of crime entails a need for a strong and central social sector with which to make allies. Thus, in order to outflank the current social fragmentation, an artificial short cut is provided.

An implicit class analysis?

The realists suggest a precise differentiation of the victims of crime and introduce factors such as vulnerability, relative damage and subjective experience. They stress that the impact of crime is very different for different victims: '£50 stolen from an OAP is very different from £50 stolen from Woolworths' (Lea and Young, 1984: 268). In order to vindicate their politics, as we have seen, they underline how crime is disruptive to the less privileged areas and hampers the processes of solidarity in working class communities. In this way they make it very clear what social group they intend to represent.

It has to be acknowledged that this is consistent with what Young emphasized some ten years ago, when he elaborated a coherent critique of 'left idealism' for

> it plays down the impact of working-class crime against the working class; it maximises the anti-working-class effects of ruling-class crime, while at the same time stressing its endemic nature. (Young, 1979: 54)

Nevertheless, it has to be noted that a 'class-oriented' search for legitimacy is among the aims of both radical and realist criminologists. The former, during the 1970s, would record the demands of the working class and would analyse them in order to decode their real needs. But real needs would often be deduced without analysing the demands through which they were expressed. In this, the radical criminologists would act pedagogically, or would avail themselves of a 'maieutic' role vis-à-vis the working class. The realists, on the other hand, resolve the problem by

> simplifying it: the demands *are* needs. If they are not, it is the task of the criminologist to separate fantasy from reality by mobilizing the 'popular consciousness'. (Pitch, 1986: 283)

Tamar Pitch argues that the realists are aware of the current social fragmentation, but are anxious to recompose it, so that they end up by postulating common needs for very diverse subjects. Instead of devoting themselves to the appraisal of this fragmentation and to the understanding of its richness, they pursue the task of rebuilding an homogeneous but imaginary community.

In fact, there seems to be an awareness among the realists that crime control policies have often been formulated in the name of one of the most overused and underdefined concepts in sociology: the community. They have pointed out the implicit functionalism associated with the term 'community', in which crime and disorder are seen as exogenous forces and the 'criminal' is assumed to be an outsider (Lea, 1986; Matthews, 1987). And yet one cannot avoid the feeling that, when underlining the predicament of the working class in high crime-rate areas, the realists are not clear enough as to what sector of the working class they are referring. They imply a notion of working class centred on values such as ethical integrity, productivity, social merit and fairness. One is induced to think that what they describe as a neat divide between offenders and victims corresponds to a similar divide between legality and illegality.

It is almost needless to be reminded that in cities like London the borders between legal, semi-legal and illegal activities are, especially in some areas, far from distinct. Thus the role of victim and offender can even be interchanged during the same day, whereas a large number of people commute periodically from semi-legal or illegal activities to legal ones. This characteristic derives from the enduring difficulties of implementing industrial discipline and morality within the city (Stedman-Jones, 1976, Fraser, 1984).

Picking on these ambiguities in the class analysis of the realists, Pitch has seen in their arguments an attempt to recompose the working class as collective actor through austerity and morality. 'The English cannot talk about austerity, they have already got a lot of it; they talk about morality, very much like our own traditional Communists, and implicitly refer to the morality of the traditional English working class' (Pitch, 1986: 286).

The realist may be aware of the inadequacy of the traditional notions of working class, but they neither make it very clear, nor do they infer consistent policies from it. On one occasion they have made reference to the new urban movements which have called forth new forms of mutuality and cooperation (Matthews, 1987). But again, this assumption, like a mere statement of intent, has not resulted in theoretical and practical proposals.

Traditional morality makes a surreptitious return in the claims that 'the working class is a victim of crime from all directions' and that 'crime is a demoralising force within the community' (Lea and Young, 1984: 269). On this specific point the critique put forward by Hobbs can be easily endorsed:

> By concentrating almost exclusively on intra-class crime, left realism is in danger of going the same way as its predecessors. For it is essential to stress the variety of criminal opportunities that are available to the working class and how, on occasions, these opportunities can enhance rather than encumber inner city life. (Hobbs, 1988: 13)

As we have seen before, 'crime as work' is not contemplated in the realist paradigm, nor is there included a notion of crime as 'service delivery'. Consequently, their emphasis on the victims has caused an overt neglect of the offenders, and their 'moral and material' economy. The square of crime of the realists is thereby reduced to a triangle.

The fifth vertex

The realists attribute a high degree of subjectivity both to victims and offenders. The former are granted individualized vulnerability and perceptions of crime and its impact. The latter are given the free will to make moral choices. It is curious how the realists do not attribute the same subjectivity to themselves. Their square of crime should instead evolve into a *pentagon*, the fifth vertex being occupied by the *observers*.

Scholars like Morin have argued for the development of a 'sociology of the sociologists' because their view on the social phenomena and the influence that their perception exercises on them cannot be underestimated (Morin, 1984). Giddens, in turn, has analysed the relationship between actor and observer in terms of their active constitution of frames of meaning whereby they organize their experience.

> The conceptual schemes of the social sciences therefore express a *double hermeneutic*, relating both to entering and grasping the frames of meaning involved in the production of social life by lay actors, and reconstituting these within the new frames of meaning involved in technical conceptual schemes. [...] The appropriation of technical concepts and theories invented by social scientists can turn them into constituting elements of that very 'subject-matter' they are coined to characterize, and by that token *alter* the context of their application. (Giddens, 1976: 79)

It is worth noting that some criminologists are well aware of their position as non-neutral observers and, consistently, point out that the task of resolving the problem of 'crime' is not so easily acceptable, nor is it among the aims of criminology. An approach strictly focused on the mission of resolving problematic situations may in fact obstruct an understanding of their scope and dimensions. It is for this reason that even prominent criminologists reject official offers of work in the field of rehabilitation, but orient their activity towards the safeguard of offenders' and prisoners' rights (Bandini and Gatti, 1986). It is also for this reason that some criminologists vindicate their function in the field as that of helping 'the criminals' to develop their own identity. The task here is not that of imposing on them norms of conduct vis-à-vis the official norms, but that of favouring in them norms of inter-action which may help the subjects identify themselves in social relations. What is meant by identity is the capacity of the actors to recognize as their own the consequences of their actions. This is regarded as the main problem for most subjects, not only for 'criminals': a more substantial problem than people's failure to comply with the official laws (Melucci, 1982; Pisapia, 1987).

The addition of a fifth vertex in the square of crime suggests a final critical note which is relevant not only to criminology, but to all sociological sub-disciplines. In order to stop the involution of sociology into mere social technology, Norbert Elias called for an increase in its degree of detachment. He advocates that the social sciences are too involved in that they are centred on synchronic, immediate and urgent situations (Elias, 1987). This sense of urgency hinders the under-standing of the historical dimensions of social actions. In narrowing their horizons, the sociologists prioritize immediate contingencies because 'they are not less influenced than ordinary people by their own ideas and prejudices' (Elias, 1987: 212). They see the social problems as part of their own problems, or as a threat to their lifestyle or their status. Their ideas are affected by heteronomous evaluations, that is to say by those evaluations which are external from the 'science' they represent, but are constructed through a personal participation in the conflicts they are supposedly studying. This leads to a circular accumu-lation of involvement: sociology is imbibed in fear, it is animated by short-term tasks and its knowledge ends up enhancing yet higher degrees of fear.

It has been lamented that there has yet to be produced an intensive history of the discipline either in terms of its internal development or of its social effects (Garland, 1985). This failure of criminology to reflect upon its own knowledge has created a situation where the role of theory in affecting its object of study is not properly realized.

Sociology should evolve into self-therapy for the sociologists, whereby they reconstruct their own history and analyse the social dynamic of their alleged knowledge (Bourdieu, 1987). This self-therapy should also be aimed at another malaise of the social sciences: the obsessive need to identify necessary relations, to draw scientific schemes of prediction in situations which are often arbitrary and unpredictable. If social actions respond to a practical logic and strategies take shape in changing patterns of interaction, so sociology should be content with descriptions which convey the same *flou*, the same vagueness that underlies the ordinary relationships of people with the world.

Conclusion

In conclusion, I would suggest that realist criminology has partly 'evaded the real'. To summarize:

There are problems the realists are aware of and succeed in resolving. One of these regards the shortcomings of radical criminology, which is also their main focus of criticism. They have succeeded in drawing attention back from the institutional responses to crime to those situations subjectively experienced by people as crime, from the mechanisms of artificial production of social panic to the mechanisms which, in social interactions, 'realistically' produce harm.

Secondly, there are problems the realists are aware of but fail to resolve. Among these are the problems concerning victimization, of which they hold a limited and selective view. They neglect those dimensions of victimization which involve ordinary people in their relationships with corporations, central and local authorities. They also overlook the notion that some offenders are themselves victims in that they constitute 'labour' in entrepreneurial-type criminal activities. The need is felt for a more accurate political economy of crime and a more comprehensive aetiology, which in their elaborations only cover specific types of crime, namely street crime.

Thirdly, their class analysis lends itself to ambiguities which arise from the crude division they see between legal and illegal behaviours. More specifically, the sector of the working class they claim to represent and whose interest they advocate seems only to be that which holds traditional English working-class values such as legality, ethical integrity, productivity, austerity and a sense of fair play.

There is finally a problem of which they seem largely unaware. This regards the role played by theory itself in the way crime is depicted. The realists lack the kind of reflexivity which would be necessary to explain the social condition of the existence of their own discipline and its role in constructing and shaping social problems. They do not consider how their own subjectivity and their own role may influence their 'realistic' depiction of social phenomena.

Some of these shortcomings, I believe, are due to their being both inside and outside the trends experienced by current criminology which I outlined at the beginning of this chapter. Their being 'inside' the institutions prevents them from widening their terrain of research and consequently their domain of knowledge.

References

Bandini, T. and Gatti, U. (1986) 'La crisi del paradigma etiologico', *Criminologia*, 13: 1–28.

Baratta, A. (1982) *Criminologia critica e critica del diritto penale*. Bologna: Il Mulino.

Baudrillard, J. (1978) *A l'ombre des majorités silencieuses ou la fin du social*. Paris: Utopie.

Bourdieu, P. (1987) *Choses Dites*. Paris: Les Editions de Minuit.

Box, S. (1987) *Recession, Crime and Punishment*. London: Macmillan.

Cacciari, M. (1978) *Dialettica e critica del politico*. Milan: Feltrinelli.

Christie, N. (1982) *Limits to Pain*. Oxford: Martin Robertson.

Cohen, S. and Young, J. (1981) *The Manufacture of News*. London: Constable-Sage.

Crawford, A., Jones, T., Woodhouse, T. and Young, J. (1990) *Second Islington Crime Survey*. Enfield: Centre for Criminology, Middlesex Polytechnic.

de Leo, G. (1986) 'Il crimine come problema e la sua spiegazione: nuovo realismo e oltre', *Dei Delitti e delle Pene*, 3: 453–67.

Elias, N. (1987) *Involvement and Detachment*. Oxford: Blackwell.

Fattah, A. (ed.) (1986) *From Crime Policy to Victim Policy*. London: Macmillan.

Fraser, D. (1984) *The Evolution of the British Welfare State*. London: Macmillan.

Garland, D. (1985) *Punishment and Welfare. A History of Penal Strategies*. Aldershot: Gower.

Giddens, A. (1976) *New Rules of Sociological Method*. London: Hutchinson.

Hobbs, D. (1988) *Doing the Business*. Oxford: OUP.

Jones, T., MacLean, B. and Young, J. (1986) *The Islington Crime Survey*. Aldershot: Gower.

Kamenka, E. and Tay, A. (1975) 'Beyond bourgeois individualism: the contemporary crisis in law and legal ideologies', in E. Kamenka and R.S. Neals (eds), *Feudalism, Capitalism and Beyond*. London: Edward Arnold.

Kinsey, R., Lea, J. and Young, J. (1986) *Losing the Fight against Crime*. Oxford: Blackwell.

Lea, J. (1986) *Towards Social Prevention: The Crisis in Crime Prevention Policy*. Enfield: Middlesex Polytechnic.

Lea, J. and Young, J. (1984) *What is to be Done about Law and Order?* Harmondsworth: Penguin.

Matthews, R. (1987) 'Taking realist criminology seriously' *Contemporary Crises*, 11: 371–401.

Matthews, R. (ed.) (1988) *Informal Justice?* London: Sage.

Mawby, R.I. and Gill, M.L. (1987) *Crime Victims. Needs, Services and the Voluntary Sector*. London: Tavistock.

Mayhew, P., Elliott, D. and Dowds, L. (1989) *The 1988 British Crime Survey*. London: HMSO.

Melucci, A. (1982) *Identita' ed azione collettiva*. Milano: Feltrinelli.

Morin, E. (1984) *Sociologie*. Paris: Fayard.

Painter, K., Lea, J., Woodhouse, T. and Young, J. (1989) *Hammersmith and Fulham Crime and Policing Survey*. Enfield: Middlesex Polytechnic.

Pearce, F. and Tombs, S. (1992) 'Realism and corporate crime', in R. Matthews and J. Young (eds), *Issues in Realist Criminology*. London: Sage.

Pisapia, G.V. (1987) 'E' possibile una clinica criminologica?', *Criminologia*, 17: 3–18.

Pitch, T. (1986) 'Viaggio attorno alla criminologia: discutendo con i realisti', *Dei Delitti e delle Pene*, 3: 469–89.

Ruggiero, V. (1986) 'La droga come merce', *Criminologia*, 5–6: 20–35.

Ruggiero, V. (1989) 'An encounter with realist criminology', in B. Rolston and M. Tomlinson (eds), *Justice and Ideology. Strategies for the 1990s*. Belfast: EGSDSC.

Ryan, M. and Ward, T. (1989) *Privatization and the Penal System*. Milton Keynes: Open University Press.

Stedman-Jones, G. (1976) *Outcast London*. Harmondsworth: Penguin.

Sutherland, E. (1940) 'White collar crime', *American Sociological Review*, 5: 1–12.

Tronti, M. (1976) *Sull'autonomia del politico*. Milan: Feltrinelli.

Williams, R. (1976) *Keywords. A Vocabulary of Culture and Society*. London: Fontana.

Winkel, W. (1987) 'Response generalisation in crime prevention campaigns', *British Journal of Criminology*, 2: 155–73.

Wright, M. and Galaway, B. (1989) *Mediation and Criminal Justice. Victims, Offenders and the Community*. London: Sage.

Young, J. (1971) *The Drugtakers*. London: Paladin.

Young, J. (1988a) 'Radical criminology: the emergence of a competing paradigm', *British Journal of Criminology*, 28: 159–83.

Young, J. (1988b) 'Risk of crime and fear of crime: a realist critique of survey-based assumptions', in M. Maguire and J. Pointing (eds), *Victims of Crime. A New Deal?* Milton Keynes: Open University Press.

Young, J. (1988c) 'Deviance', in P. Worsley (ed.), *The New Introducing Sociology*. Harmondsworth: Penguin.

6 Rediscovering crime

John Lowman

The left realist project

While the formal articulation of a left realism did not occur until 1984 with the publication of John Lea and Jock Young's *What is to be Done about Law and Order?*, the position they articulated was already immanent in Young's papers on 'Working class criminology' (1975) and 'Left idealism and reformism' (1979), and was given important impetus by Ian Taylor's (1981) *Law and Order: Arguments for Socialism.*[1] By now, as a result of the energetic writing of Richard Kinsey, John Lea, Jock Young, Roger Matthews and others, the realist agenda is well known. It proceeds from the argument that the first phases of critical anglophone criminology so overemphasized the analytic importance of state social control institutions and mechanisms of deviance definition that the realists of the new right appeared to be the only constituency able and available to address widespread public concerns about crime victimization. For Lea and Young (1984), the main impetus for the articulation of left realism arose from the need 'to redress the balance in radical thinking' which tended to minimize the importance of 'working-class crime' by pointing to the putatively more weighty crimes of the powerful, and by treating street crime either as a diversion from class struggle, or as a vehicle for marketing news.

Lea and Young (1984) fault left idealism for treating crime as an epiphenomenon, with the criminal – conceived of as a sort of socialist homunculus or proto-revolutionary – being viewed as determined and blameless, punishment as unwarranted or amplificatory. In relating crime to other aspects of social formations, discussion of the social formations tended to dominate the discourse. From this perspective any talk of criminal justice reform is largely irrelevant, since if crime is a consequence of capitalism, the only way to deal with it is to bring about the demise of capitalism. In conceiving political action this way, crime has been effectively exiled from much critical analysis. The victim did not enter the picture at all, except as yet another generic victim of capitalism. The problem with this kind of formulation for

Lea and Young is that it is simply the inverse of the conservative position in which crime is a wilful act and the law-abiding must be protected by the institution of punishment; thus while conservative criminology portrays it as an unalterable consequence of social structure, left idealism portrays it as an unalterable consequence of social structure.

Alternatively for Lea and Young's left realism, crime is shaped, but not straightforwardly determined, by social structure, and it is a social problem because it compounds other problems of capitalism. Most of all it is a problem for marginal populations for whom street crime is a serious matter; indeed, the key characteristic of street crime from this perspective is the general symmetry of victims and offenders. Thus left realism reasserts the seriousness of street crime, acknowledges that consensus over a core group of laws does exist, and advocates various kinds of criminal justice reform and crime prevention strategy as the most immediate goals of a socialist criminology (Kinsey et al., 1986; Lea and Young, 1984; Matthews and Young, 1986; Taylor 1981). As much as anything else, left realism provides a *critical victimology* in which local surveys (Jones et al., 1986) dealing with crime victimization, fear of crime and attitudes to the police – adaptations of and additions to the familiar tools of technicist and administrative criminology – assume a pointedly political edge.

The purpose of this chapter is to reflect upon and offer something of a supportive critique of the left realist manifesto – supportive, that is, of its demand that critical theory take 'crime' victimization seriously, but critical in that it treats with suspicion any return to the terrain of criminal justice. The discussion proceeds by examining Stanley Cohen's (1987, 1988) reassertion of certain moral and potentially anti-utilitarian values against the realist project. But although concurring with Cohen's anti-criminological sentiments and disquiet with utilitarianism, this chapter also supports the position that the protection of certain rights cannot be achieved without some centralized system of codified norms (laws by any other name) and norm enforcement not just within the nation state, but internationally as well. A brief examination of the politics of prostitution in one urban setting is used to identify some of the difficulties associated with the decentralization of formal social control mechanisms whether it be complete (abolitionism)[2] or partial (left realism). This is not ultimately an argument against the democratization of criminal justice institutions, far from it, but a caution that populism and particularism might not help to achieve social democracy. This example also helps to identify some of the difficulties associated with developing a realist perspective on punishment.

The appeal of anti-criminology and the abolitionist sentiment

It would be a mistake to conceive left realism as it has developed thus far as yet another inversion, this time of left idealism or of what has been characterized as the 'revisionist' perspective on social control. For while left realism attempts to provide a progressive agenda for criminal justice reform, it does not do so by denying the importance of white-collar, corporate and government crime[3] or by ignoring the social reaction to perceived deviance; rather it points to the theoretical and political consequences of approaches which deal with nothing but the crimes of the powerful, or the actions of rule makers and enforcers. Nevertheless, as it currently stands, its position on arcane crime remains an unfinished project by virtue of receiving little attention in the actual research that has been carried out to date under the banner of left realism. And while the general claims of Young and his colleagues have been criticized for creating far too much of a caricature of developments in critical criminology (Ward and Ryan, 1989; Dekeseredy and Schwartz, 1991), and as being somewhat unfair to radical organizations standing outside the formal British political structure (Ward and Ryan, 1989), most progressive thinkers commenting on the left realist agenda have found it difficult to reject outright the appeal to take 'crime' victimization seriously. The idea that any progressive criminology ought to incorporate a critical victimology, whether it relates to victims of what we call 'crime' or people ending up on the wrong side of what Hulsman (1986) calls 'problematic situations', finds few opponents. What is much more controversial is how much stock any progressive agenda for dealing with 'crime', or whatever we call it, should put in a formal state controlled criminal justice system for attaining its goals. It is at this point that left realism and some of its progressive critics part company.

Reaffirming some ideals By virtue of appearing on the stage of criminological history as a particular kind of polemic, left realism has been interpreted as losing too much of value in pointing to the weaknesses of more idealist leftist perspectives. In the process left realism runs the risk of losing the vision of radical alternatives to criminal justice, or at least of identifying and promoting alternative principles on which criminal justice might be based. It is its tendency to reject or downplay the destructuring visions that inspired the anti-criminology of the 1970s and its return to the formal terrain of traditional criminology, its 'defensive formalism' (cf. Cain, 1985) or 'radical regression' (Cohen, 1987), that produce cause for concern. One question is whether the treading of the traditional terrain of criminal justice as a short-term political expedient requires the whole-sale rejection of longer-term deconstructionist ideals. Much more problematic is the question of whether short-term expedients can be invoked without thwarting long-term political goals.

While Cohen has become one of the most influential commentators on social control institutions[4] he certainly does not commit (nor does he stand accused of) the 'thought crime' of left idealism. Cohen's work is of particular relevance to the articulation of left realism first, because it presents something of an (in some ways complementary) alternative in the form of *moral pragmatism* (1985: 252) – a view which asserts a series of values as deserving in their own right as opposed to being desirable for their utility – and second, because he finds it necessary to reassert these values against left realism. Moral pragmatism is Cohen's guiding criterion for evaluating community control:

> The moral element affirms doing good and doing justice as values in themselves. By 'doing good' I mean not just individual concern about private troubles but a commitment to the socialist reform of the public issues which cause those troubles. By 'doing justice' I mean not equity or retribution but the sense of rightness and fairness for the collective good ... (i.e.) utilitarian aims such as reducing crime should not be achieved at the cost of sacrificing cherished values.... The pragmatic element stands against all forms of premature theoretical and political closure.... (1985: 252–3)

Although Cohen refers to the left realist manifesto as 'clear and convincing' (1987: 368), he laments its renunciation of the anti-criminological sentiments that spawned the sociology of deviance, gave considerable impetus to the initial phases of critical criminology, and provided the theoretical foundation for what he calls the de-structuring movements of the 1960s – delegalization, decarceration, deinstitutionalization, decriminalization, etc. In evaluating left realism, Cohen's purpose is to reaffirm the values of the anti-criminology that originally broke from the technicist mainstream by, for example, attacking structures of control and centralized state power, by being suspicious of expertise and classification, and by moving criminology beyond the criminal event. Cohen (1987) interprets left realism as an almost complete reversal of the anti-criminological enterprise; for left realism criminal justice is to be colonized, established control mechanisms are to be utilized, police and law are to be mobilized rather than demystified. Following E.P. Thompson (1977), left realists evince a renewed faith in the law. For them, the formal equality of law is much more than an ideological veneer covering the rot of substantive inequality. As a mechanism of resistance, not just an instrument of domination, it is to be defended as a potential site of conflict resolution.

Thus, while left realism and Cohen's vision of destructuring share a commitment to decentralized systems of power, what Cohen finds problematic is the realist's ultimate reliance on centralized state power:

> The return to the terrain of the traditional criminal justice model ... is not just to abandon the vision of decentralized community control but to renounce a major weapon for creating an alternative criminology.

> You cannot, that is, have it both ways: statist criminal law and decentralization. To be realistic about law and order must mean to be unrealistic (that is, imaginative) about the possibilities of order without law. To take decentralization seriously means you must be an abolitionist. (1987: 374)

Ultimately the logic of the assertion that you cannot have it both ways seems obvious enough. But are things really this clear-cut, this uncompromising?

What's in a name? While left realists argue that critical criminology needs to take crime victimization seriously and must at some level relate to public discourse, they would apparently not disagree that a progressive perspective which aims to enlighten criminal justice policy must also be able to stand in opposition to that discourse. To do otherwise is to encourage the reification of the concept of 'crime'. Some critics have worried that by taking crime seriously realism does just this. But how much would abolishing the concept of crime in the way that Hulsman (1986) suggests actually deal with the problem of reification? It would seem that this problem is not limited to the notion of 'crime' since, without a significant change in the relationship between words and things in western language, any concept or system of concepts we might choose to designate objects of censure and denunciation is potentially subject to the same sort of reification. And as Lea points out (1987: 361), if we were to adopt Hulsman's abolitionist strategy of talking about 'problematic situations' rather than 'crimes', such situations would still be subject to shifting processes of power and communication, and the person studying them cannot stand outside this process. The observation that not all problematic situations are crimes and not all crimes are problematic situations simply points to the general conflict about what should be censured and by what mechanism.

To be weighed against the disadvantages created by the state's categorization of certain kinds of problematic situations as crimes are the seemingly inescapable advantages of a centrally defined code of conduct, criminal or otherwise. While the criminal law of contemporary capitalist societies may be far too extensive, what would replace it as a mechanism for identifying acts which the collectivity could justifiably use force to prevent? If legal codes were to be abolished, how would certain basic rights even be expressed and how would they be safeguarded? If the state is to disappear, what mechanisms would replace the regulatory functions of administrative and civil law in complex large-scale societies – or are we simply going to allow unmaintained jumbo jets to plummet into our midst? If it is agreed that collectivities of nation states share certain interests (relating to pollution, exploitation of natural resources, and a host of other things) what mechanism other than a system of international law could express collective expectations about appropriate conduct? What institutions other than 'governments' might conspire to produce international regulations? Once some code of conduct is in place, how does one avoid instituting a specialized 'police' when some of the issues at stake, particularly pressing environmental problems, are so fundamental that they are implicated in our very survival?

As much as anything else law is a categorization of expectations and no matter how imperfect its operation it is indispensable in this sense (especially when the expectations relate to technically complex issues like pollution and where regulations would require highly specialized knowledge to enforce them). In the short term the main issues would thus seem to be not only about democratizing decision making but also about the types of regulation that are appropriate for different types of conduct and how rule makers and enforcers are to be made accountable. It is difficult to see how flight from the concept of 'crime' is going to help deal with some of these issues.

Reconciling short- and long-term interests

> (T)he outlook is poor for the basic social changes that the left has in mind, and in any case, no one on the left has proposed a clear set of long-range strategies for coping with crime. Unless we decide to opt out entirely on crime-control issues, we are going to have to overcome our traditional reluctance to take positions on short term strategies. All too often, we have allowed our awareness of social injustice in the operation of the criminal justice system to immobilize us. To become involved in crime-control policy does indeed incur the risk of dirtying one's hands. But the alternative of allowing the right to run amok also raises ethical issues. Dirty hands are preferable to having no hands at all in the formulation of criminal justice policy. (Rafter, 1986: 18).

Against the visionary arguments of abolitionism and long-range blueprints for socialism are more immediate demands to do something about particular kinds of crime. The idea of abolishing law and the state can provide no solace for the sometimes long-lasting distress of the crime victim. It seems unlikely in countries like Australia, Canada, England and the US, in the short term at least, that criminal justice will disappear. If one has any interest in dealing with the anguish of the crime victim or in realigning the targets of criminal justice (to include polluters, for example) one has to confront criminal justice issues, at least partly, on traditional terrain.

The most poignant demands to take victimization seriously have come from various feminist constituencies precisely at a time when talk about 'widening nets' preoccupied (mostly male) students of social control. On the one side are fears about the normalizing power of the state and the balance of class interests that it represents. On the other side are a variety of images of expanding crime rates, and of general categories of crime victimization all too often ignored by the criminal justice system, particularly widespread violence against women. Against the history of the state's lack of intervention in violence against women it seems difficult to object to the notion that, at least in the short term, the criminal justice system ought to be used to curtail rape, and that the visual record of an actual sex-murder – the so-called 'snuff' movie – should not be available for public consumption. And while one may be well aware of the normalizing and reificatory capacity of discourse about crime, it is difficult to see how the re-designation of rape as a 'problematic situation' offers any particular advantage. In large part it was this concern about the criminal victimization of women that paved the way for the sort of critical victimology that has emerged from left realism. But these developments still leave many questions about the role of the state in facilitating preferred kinds of social change. Feminists disagree over the extent to which criminal law should be used to intervene in gender relations (there is, for example, considerable ambivalence about the regulation of both prostitution and pornography)[5] such that it is as important to recognize the considerable disagreements among different feminisms as it is to understand their common bonds. Obviously these kinds of issues are not specific to feminism.

In a more general sense a variety of arguments need to be weighed against any desire to expand the net of criminal justice. Foremost among these is the realization that utilitarian projects in criminology have often been used as means of gaining better control over certain sections of the population rather than maximizing justice, and that arguments for control in one domain often become the rationale for increased control over disenfranchised populations in others. The problem with short-range solutions for Cohen is that they do not ultimately challenge the normalizing power of the state; the state's power of definition must always be susceptible to challenge. But I can see no reason why the desire to take certain kinds of crime seriously – that is, to adopt utilitarian and strategic goals – necessarily means relinquishing deconstructionst objectives wholesale. It is worth noting in this respect that in outlining moral pragmatism as a system of values in which 'utilitarian and strategic considerations should, where possible, be secondary to attaining these values for their own sake and whatever their other results', Cohen does not deny that strategic goals are often justifiable. What he downplays here is the idea that cherished values and strategic goals might often coincide. Thus in saying that while he prefers to be pragmatic about short-term possibilities, he remains 'genuinely utopian about constructing long term alternatives' (1985: 252), Cohen would seem to have identified a ground where his moral pragmatism and left realism, despite its retreat to the terrain of criminal justice, can find some common purpose. Short-term goals, while having to conform to certain predetermined values, ought to be realistic in the sense that they are politically feasible. Long-term goals can be genuinely utopian. In this sense you *can* have it both ways, although the problem of how to prevent short-term strategies from being coopted in a way that thwarts long-term goals still remains (indeed, given their preoccupation with immediate criminal justice reform one wonders what some of the longer-term goals of left realism might look like). In that it espouses a minimalist stance on punishment left realism can be seen to conform to some of the values that Cohen espouses, particularly the minimization of pain that is inflicted in the process of punishment. But the realist concern with victimization also serves as a reminder that crime, like punishment, can be about the infliction of pain. If we are concerned about minimizing the pain that is associated with punishment, it seems difficult to argue that we should not also be concerned with minimizing the pain that arises from 'crime' (be it the result of a defective petrol tank, the Dalkon Shield, a sexual assault, or a robbery).

Arguing from a slightly different perspective, Lea (1987: 365) flatly rejects Cohen's assertion that realism's response to the decentralization dilemma is simply to retreat back to formal criminal justice; whether this is clear in the texts Cohen is reacting to (Lea and Young, 1984; Young, 1986) is another matter. Rather, Lea claims, it aspires to offer a new form of relation between criminal justice and community-based alternatives, and he also cautions against regression into earlier positions. The left realist strategy is for the creation of a system where there is interpenetration of centralized and decentralized institutions. Thus the retention of a system of criminal justice would not require a singular approach to 'crime'. It would be supplemented by a 'wide variety of mediation, dispute settlement, legal advice provision and crisis intervention agencies apart from the police, and of a localized and decentralized character' (Lea, 1987: 367). Thus in some cases dispute settlement *should* be left in the hands of those people immediately involved; their conflict should remain their property, to use

Christie's (1977) imagery. In other instances it cannot remain private property in this sense since it is not clear who the 'immediate' participants are (one such example relating to street prostitution will be discussed below), or in situations where the collectivity has as much or more interest in the 'problem situation' as the immediate participants (sexism, racism, ecological matters, etc).

The practical course that left realism charts through these waters involves the development of a system of centralized criminal justice agencies which are, as far as possible, localized and democratized: 'If the laws are enacted centrally then the locality is the best place to decide which are the most important priorities and how they should be enforced.' If is thus the 'discretionary element of central agencies which can be as far as possible localized and democratized' (Lea, 1987: 368).

While all critical realist writing calls for historically and culturally specific analysis, it would seem that this model for the interplay of state law and community justice is not intended to be applicable only to the specific context of Britain's cities, but is being offered as a much more general model of the way that centralized and decentralized institutions can interpenetrate. But here we come to one of the main problems raised by utilitarian reasoning. What if 'democratic' participation of the sort envisaged here produces utilitarian or particularistic responses which run against such values as 'minimal' policing and 'minimal' punishment? And just how much participation at the local level might one expect to garner in the operation of social control and dispute resolution mechanisms?

Social democracy and popular justice

With an immediately practical agenda in hand Kinsey et al. (1986) reject the overwhelming air of pessimism characterizing much radical criminological discourse and contend that 'only an informed socialist policy, involving the restructuring of the relations between police, local community and local government, is likely ever to make our cities tolerable places for working class people to live' (1986: 36). This call for the radical democratization of policing is based on the suggestion that policing cannot be more effective without the complicity of the community. For, they suggest, it is precisely community alienation from the police and the police from the community (a mutual alienation accentuated by the transition from a 'consensus' to a 'military' style of policing inner-city Britain) that leads to escalating crime rates: 'We have created in this country a criminal justice system which alienates precisely that section of the population which would otherwise be the main source of information about crime and the public bedrock of successful policing' (Kinsey et al., 1986: 48). Among the many issues that these suggested strategies raise, two stand out. The first concerns the faith Kinsey and his colleagues place in 'the community', whatever that may mean (cf. Cohen, 1985: 116–27); Iadicola, 1986), for producing democratic policing; the second concerns the appeal to heed local interests when it comes to policing but not when it comes to punishment. The second issue points to what would appear to be one Achilles heel of left realism; that is its position on punishment.

The 'community' and policing priorities   In pondering the merits of an approach which tries to achieve the goals of social democracy by appealing to popular concerns, one is left wondering why community control of police policy might not lead to the same forms of xenophobia and racism that already characterize police–community relations in inner-city Britain. The posing of this question is not meant to suggest that the advocates of democratic-socialist policing policies are unaware of the problems that community control raises. Kinsey et al. (1986: 102) acknowledge that certain neighbourhood crime prevention initiatives might exacerbate racism, not alleviate it, and that it would be easy for certain interest groups to dominate decision making. This is why maximum participation of community members in crime prevention initiatives is essential to any model of community control. But how likely is it that the democratization of policing would result in the kind of participation envisaged?

The experience of community crime prevention schemes in North America certainly leaves little room to be optimistic. Krajick's (1979) review of crime prevention programme reveals that they usually experience very low levels of participation and that, from a police perspective, they are often little more than half-hearted public relations efforts. This might be because, as Kinsey et al. note (1986: 117), the modern discourse on crime prevention treats the public as an agency for providing information, not as a source of demands; crime prevention and community involvement are *management techniques* in which the views of the community are rarely represented.[6] It may also be that lack of participation in crime prevention programmes reflects widespread apathy about community initiatives generally. This, in itself, may not be a problem if one follows Kinsey et al.'s argument that locally elected police authorities must become the public voice of policing policy (1986: 175) in a system which maintains police accountability to formal law (1986: 189). But what if the process of democratizing decisions about policing priorities does not produce egalitarian social control institutions? What if locally elected police authorities were to demand exclusionary and punitive policies, some of which might adversely affect other localities? One illustration of these kinds of problems can be provided by a short digression into issues surrounding street prostitution policing in Vancouver, Canada.

A vignette: community responses to street prostitution Vancouver has been the site of considerable lobby group pressure over the past 10 years for something to be done about the street prostitution problem which has been widely perceived as getting out of control in most Canadian cities since a 1978 ruling of the Supreme Court of Canada. This ruling is said to have rendered unenforceable the 'soliciting' law which made it an offence to 'solicit in a public place for the purpose of prostitution' (Lowman, 1989a).[7] While there are all sorts of reasons to suggest that 'what went wrong' with prostitution law[8] is much more complicated than this, the reaction to the street prostitution problem over the past 10 years is useful for raising a variety of questions about the role of 'the community' in producing democratic crime policies.

In Vancouver prior to 1970 street prostitution was mainly confined to two 'skid row'-type areas in the downtown commercial district. For a variety of reasons[9] street prostitution broke out of these traditional locations at some time in the late 1960s and a new 'stroll' was established in the West End, the residential high-rise district located immediately to the west of the downtown core.

In 1981 a group of local residents formed CROWE (the Concerned Residents of the West End) with the single purpose of trying to rid the area of street prostitutes and their customers. A variety of strategies were devised to suppress street prostitution in the area but not until 1984, when the Provincial Government of British Columbia issued civil nuisance injunctions against prostitutes working in the West End, was there any measure of success. While this strategy did achieve the particularistic goal of clearing this 'hot spot' of prostitutes, it did so only by displacing them to other localities, one of which was the working-class residential neighbourhood of Mount Pleasant. As was the case in the West End, a group of residents was quick to organize against street prostitution in their neighbourhood.

In 1985 the federal government revised the street prostitution law to make it an offence to communicate in a public place for the purpose of prostitution. But by the summer of 1986 when it became apparent that this new law was also failing to curb the street prostitution trade, Mount Pleasant residents once again began lobbying the federal government to toughen its stance.

The police response to escalating problems in Mount Pleasant was to establish a series of special prostitution task forces each summer from 1986 to 1989. Task force personnel adopted a strategy of 'zero tolerance' in order to harass prostitutes and customers out of the area (men cruising the streets were stopped and ticketed for any traffic violations they might be committing; prostitutes were routinely sub-jected to identity checks, and given littering and jaywalking tickets whenever possible). While these efforts appear to have been very successful, again the result was the displacement of prostitution rather than its suppression (Lowman, 1989a: 88–92).[10]

One of the areas Mount Pleasant prostitutes moved to was Strath-cona, the lowest income neighbourhood in Vancouver, and one in which prostitution has been a familiar fixture throughout its history. Up to 1986 street prostitution was confined to a commercial district close to Vancouver's skid row, but since then has spread into resi-dential streets. At some neighbourhood meetings the familiar demands 'to get tough with prostitutes were heard, but were initially resisted by a group of key individuals who insisted that if prostitutes were going to be moved, they should be given some indication of where to move to. A map was drawn up and distributed to prostitutes requesting them to work in certain non-residential streets, and an informal arrangement made with patrol police not to hassle prostitutes who moved to those streets. But demands to remove prostitutes from the area altogether have escalated and there are signs that prostitutes are already starting to move into another neighbourhood.

Now that the federal government is considering further revisions to the street prostitution law the local mayor, police chief and anti-street prostitution lobby groups have all offered the same reason for the 'failure' of the communicating law to clear the city's streets; in-adequate sentences. The way to deal with street prostitutes and their customers, they say, is to install a more punitive regime by legislating mandatory prison sentences.

The experience of street prostitution policing in Vancouver points to several difficulties that any appeal to 'community' values may en-counter. First, it is difficult to know what 'community reactions' to prostitution actually consist of since the opinions of small but very vocal groups have dominated the discourse (in Mount Pleasant, for example, the two lobby groups that emerged to oust prostitutes never included more than about 20 members between them), although it is unlikely that many people would want to encourage street prostitution in their own neighbourhood. When the Vancouver police established a liaison committee in Mount Pleasant to facilitate community input on crime problems generally, concerns about prostitution – the most visible problem – overwhelmed all others. Indeed, the police members of this committee say that when it comes to other criminal justice issues it has been very difficult to get any community input at all (and Mount Pleasant has some of the highest official crime rates in residential Vancouver).

Secondly, for the most part, the kinds of responses of communities in Vancouver to street prostitution have been particularistic; they aim to achieve one specific goal and often without caring about the ramifications either for people in other neighbourhoods (representatives of CROWE, for example, publicly stated several times that they did not care where prostitution went as long as it left the West End) or prostitutes. When it comes to the issue of where prostitutes *should* work (prostitution itself is, after all, legal in Canada)[11] these groups are usually mute.

Thirdly, in striving single-mindedly for certain utilitarian goals anti-street prostitution lobby groups do not evince much interest in considering other objectives and principles that might be involved in the construction of criminal law. For example, those groups that refuse to confront the issue of where prostitutes ought to work apparently care little about the liberal democratic reasoning underlying the Canadian government's refusal to criminalize the acts of buying and selling sexual services in the first place; namely that sexual acts between consenting adults should not be the business of the criminal law. Any concern which can be interpreted as 'taking the side of prostitutes' generally falls by the wayside as public propriety and property values become the paramount issues. Obviously there are other issues in respect to prostitution, such as the desirability of the commodification of sexuality and the exploitation of women, which need to be taken into consideration in designing prostitution policy. These collective interests are particularly relevant to *left* realism in that they problematize the liberal notion of rights that underlies the sort of reasoning which has thus far prevented the Canadian government from criminalizing prostitution. Since these issues are dealt with more extensively elsewhere (Lowman, 1990), it is sufficient to note here that it does not seem that one can have it both ways; if prostitution is to remain legal *and* residents are to be protected from the nuisances attributed to the street prostitution trade someone has to deal with the issue of where prostitution ought to be located.

Fourthly, local interest groups would be highly critical of any attempt to curtail their input to decisions about punishment, since they are already arguing that it is the inappropriate response of the judiciary in terms of sentencing practices that is thwarting police efforts. The question is, on what basis could one grant community participation in decisions about policing but not about punishment (a problem taken up in the final section of this chapter)?

While some of these observations point to difficulties left realism may encounter in its attempt to democratize criminal justice decision making, these difficulties would be even more pronounced for an abolitionist project. In this sense the issues discussed here tend to confirm recently expressed left realist criticisms of abolitionism. Lea

(1987), for example, rejects the abolitionist proposal for a completely substantive system of justice 'collapsed into the structure of social relations' where community and neighbourhood reconciliation mechanisms would replace criminal justice on the grounds that it would produce a very repressive and/or locally differentiated system of justice with marked disparities in norm enforcement and dispute settlement.[12] No matter what 'justice' and/or conflict resolution mechanism might be employed, there should still be some protection of the individual against capricious decision making. It is difficult to see how a complex society can avoid some general code of conduct which allows one to know in advance what forms of behaviour are sanctionable. The street prostitution example also points to the difficulty of resolving conflicts entirely at a local level when much broader principles, such as the legality of prostitution itself, are at stake. The prostitution issue also provides an example of one of the problems that Matthews (1987) identifies with Christie's (1977) proposal to make crime the exclusive property of the individuals involved; namely that crime, because of its 'profoundly social' nature, affects the collectivity, not just the individual victim. In the case of street prostitution it is social in a somewhat different sense; that is, it is not always clear who the victim and offender are since some of the nuisances associated with the street trade (such as traffic congestion and general noise) and its overall effect on a neighbourhood are not always reducible in a legal sense to a specific individual.

The punishment question In granting a rational core to popular concerns about crime and in making policing a large part of the answer to it (Kinsey et al., 1986), left realists apparently evince a certain degree of faith in the deterrent capacity of apprehension (why else would one wish to catch more criminals?), but take a minimalist stance when it comes to punishment (Young, 1987: 353). To this extent left realists would appear to reject demands for harsher treatment of most criminals – indeed, they apparently argue that we should punish less severely than we do now – even if such demands could be shown to enjoy popular support. Whether a large segment of the public does support more punitiveness is uncertain. Recent crime surveys have produced some important findings to the extent that they suggest that 'Public opinion, in Britain at least, appears to demand only a limited use of custodial sentences in cases of violence or other extremely serious offences, while in the majority of cases it advocates sanctions which provide tangible consequences for offenders and which reasonably express its disapproval' (Matthews, 1987: 395). Similarly Taylor (1981: 141) has suggested that 'popular rhetorics of justice would operate to redefine the bulk of the offences for which people are currently imprisoned as offences demanding compensation or other non-segretative responses'. But as Hunt observes, the appeal to popular justice

> ... is an open invitation to make use of exemplary punishments in response to social or moral panic. Further, it introduces the possibility of an extreme degree of variation of sentence which has been widely regarded as running contrary to a progressive penology. In any proposals for a community based justice system, it is essential to avoid any romanticization of 'the community' as necessarily rational and compassionate; the community is just as capable of irrationality and vindictiveness as any official judicial institution. (1982: 19)

Current demands in Canada for the introduction of mandatory prison sentences for street prostitutes represent one example of such a response. In other respects, attitudes to sentencing in Canada appear to be not much different from those in England, to the extent that there appears to be fairly widespread support for non-custodial sentences for property crimes (Doob, 1990). But other Canadian research indicates fairly widespread support for increasing the severity of sentences in a general sense! It turns out that there is a fairly straightforward explanation for these apparently contradictory findings, one which has important implications for any community-based criminal justice; that is, decisions based on populist concerns are only as good as the information on which those concerns are based.

A series of nationwide opinion polls have shown that the majority of respondents believed that sentences generally were too lenient; this dissatisfaction was greatest in 1983 when 80 percent of those polled expressed this belief (Doob and Roberts, 1983). But the Canadian Sentencing Commission (1987: 91) recently showed that many people are largely ignorant of the realities of sentencing and that they systematically underestimate the severity of the reaction to crime and overestimate crime seriousness by, for example, severely overestimating the relative proportion of violent as compared to propety crimes (hence the more specific examination of public attitudes to the sentences appropriate for particular types of crime yields quite different results). Presumably this is the kind of public stereotyping of crime that Young (1987: 337) would want to debunk. But the nature of public sentiments about the appropriateness of different kinds of punishment for different kinds of offenders aside, how would left realism respond to widespread public support for exemplary sentencing if it could be shown to be based upon accurate perceptions of sentences that are imposed? On what grounds, for example, could the state resist reintroduction of the death penalty in the event that there is wide popular support for its use?

Having given credence to the notion of deterrence by detection (that more efficient policing would deter offenders) does it not also implicitly feed the notion that more punishment will deter more people? The issue I want to take up here is not whether these views about police efficiency and deterrence are correct – although it is difficult to disagree with Garland (1987: 200) that Kinsey et al. (1986) 'overstate the potential of policing to reduce the incidence of criminal offences and they dramatically understate the other factors involved' – but of how a progressive politics of the left could use popular support to justify one criminal justice strategy but deny it in the case of the other. The crucial problem is that when other 'punishment' strategies are either not employed, or in the event that they are employed they do not work, utilitarian reasoning would seem to give licence to the idea that if all else fails escalating prison sentences will, at some point, have the desired effect.

   Part of the left realist rationale for a minimal use of prison is that it is massively expensive, brutalizing and counterproductive. After all, the narrowly punitive policies of right realists can hardly be said to be working, judging by increasing crime rates in Britain and the United States. But there are many reasons to doubt that increased police efficiency would, by itself, have much of an impact on levels of crime if one cannot come up with an alternative to custody which could also be justified, at least partly, on utilitarian grounds. So far about the only way out of this problem has been to reaffirm some of the principles that have always been used to justify incarceration. Matthews (1987: 393) for example, suggests that 'Instead of simply rejecting the formal justifications for punishment – whether deterrence, incapacitation or rehabilitation – we need to evaluate these justifications not at a global level but rather ask specifically which justifications apply to which sorts of offenders, for which crimes, committed under which particular conditions.' But while it makes sense to continue to attempt to find and use alternatives to incarceration and make incarceration a more relevant and constructive form of penalty when it is thought to be necessary, the question remains, how might one actually do this? Without very specific answers to this question, the principle of minimal punishment might well backfire. Ultimately, the way out of this dilemma is to create a strong link between criminal justice policy and other kinds of social policy and, ultimately, to de-emphasize the instrumental potential of punishment. On this score left realism has been criticized for concentrating too much on crime and not enough on transformative economic and social policies (Dekeseredy and Schwartz, 1991) and without an integrated and comprehensive approach, it might not end up looking much different from plain old liberalism. In this respect the reforms advocated by left realists sometimes do not end up looking very different from much that has gone before; indeed, it is not always clear what is 'left' about the criminal justice strategies that are proposed other than the rhetoric in which they are couched. And, as another reader of this literature has observed,[13] one wonders if left realism would end up being much different from certain aspects of the Fabian utilitarianism which once came under the critical scrutiny of the likes of Jock Young back in 1975 (Taylor et al., 1975: 9–14).

Conclusions: realism in a broader context

While left realism must be understood as a reaction to a particular conjunction of intellectual and political forces in Britain and has the potential to become a powerful practical force in terms of shaping Labour Party crime policy, its advocates have been careful to argue that the specifics of empirical analysis in one national context cannot be carelessly generalized to another. But I take it that this principle of historical and cultural specificity neither suggests that comparative analyses cannot be instructive, nor does it preclude generalization of theoretical, moral and certain political prescriptions. The principles of social democracy that left realism espouses, for example, particularly the call for the interpenetration of centralized and decentralized structures of decision making, would appear to be generalizable to any contemporary western capitalist society. And with Young's (1987) linking of the theoretical prerequisites of realism with the formal and substantial requirements of a 'fully social theory of deviance' as originally articulated in *The New Criminology* (Taylor et al., 1973), we see left realism moving beyond its purely reactive and polemical phase to make wider connections and re-establish a variety of theoretical elements that have thus far been downplayed. The task of showing how these various elements of a fully social theory of deviance relate to philosophical realism (cf. Keat and Urry, 1976) in a broader sense still remains.

In this chapter I have suggested that the principles of left realism and Cohen's moral pragmatism, despite Cohen's resistance to the realist colonization of the criminal justice system, are not ultimately anti-thetical. To this extent I have interpreted the utilitarian impulse of left realism as it has developed to date as being, in part, a product of its polemical character – a political posture related to the theoretical and political developments (right realism, left idealism and abolitionism) against which it emerged – and that the process of taking 'crime' victimization seriously does not require the relinquishing of certain deconstructionist principles and values.

At a more practical level, an examination of local community input to decisions about prostitution policing in Vancouver served to high-light some of the problems already acknowledged, but perhaps not adequately dealt with, by left realists involving utilitarian reasoning, especially when carried over to strategies of punishment, and that if community involvement in criminal justice decision making becomes too particularistic it might serve to undermine social democratic goals.

Ultimately the main problem facing left realism would appear to be in the way that it connects criminal justice with other kinds of social and economic policy. And even with the careful elaboration of this connection, it may be difficult for left realism to avoid becoming a sort of neo-Fabianism or relatively undisguised liberalism. But, then, after 10 years of Thatcher, Reagan and Bush, less than this might seem like a victory.

Notes

Thanks to Bob Menzies, Kim Rossmo and Simon Davis for their comments on this paper.

1. Lea and Young represent their 1984 argument as a direct response to this work. They also identify Platt (1978) as part of the realist tradition in socialist criminology.

2. Abolitionism, as represented by the contributions to the 1986 special issue of *Contemporary Crises* (10: 3–106) for example, is an amphorous sentiment which offers neither a distinct philosophy of social science nor an integrated politics; Scheerer (1986), for example, concludes that abolitionism is a 'sensitizing politic which serves to destabilize the quasi-axiomatic beliefs upon which the criminal justice system is built.'

3. Lea and Young unequivocally argue that, 'what is necessary is a double thrust against both types of crime' (1984: 73).

4. Cohen states that 'it would be a bizarre type of theory that completely ignored the possibility that the expansion of the crime control system over the past two decades . . . is a direct response to increasing official crime rates . . .' He also suggests that changes in control 'cannot explain away real structural factors that would lead one to an increased crime rate during this period' (1985: 91). Bizarre as it might be, Cohen does not, in fact, offer any analysis of changing rates of 'crime' in discussing the expansion of control.

5. There is a sizeable feminist constituency in Canada thoroughly opposed to the censorship of pornography (Burstyn, 1985).

6. It is in this respect that they are critical of Scarman's vision of police–community consultation: 'Scarman . . . advocated and made respectable a type of police–community consultation in which police are free to take notice of one section of the community at one time and another, or none, the next – with no guarantee that police priorities will necessarily reflect those of the community' (Kinsey et al., 1986: 157).

7. In terms of the evidence necessary to secure a conviction, police construed the soliciting law as only requiring them to establish that a person had, in a public place, offered a sexual service for a fee. In 1978 the Supreme Court of Canada upheld a ruling that soliciting constituted 'pressing and persistent' behaviour. This meant that in order to secure a conviction police had to establish that a prostitute had been a tangible *nuisance* in the process of offering sexual services for a fee. Vancouver police laid very few soliciting charges thereafter.

8. In Canada prostitution is technically legal, but a combination of laws makes it effectively illegal. Canadian and English prostitution laws are similar, with one key difference being that in Canada a single prostitute is not exempt from bawdy house law.

9. The details are provided by Lowman, 1986, 1989b.

10. In acknowledgement of the need to provide specific analysis, this example is not meant to suggest that these types of initiatives will always produce displacement; rather, it is an example of some of the problems that can be associated with decentralized decision making. Indeed, Matthews (1986) has suggested that prostitution may be more opportunistic than has traditionally been supposed, although it is debatable whether this conclusion can be drawn from the methodology that he employed in studying attempts to 'design out' prostitution from Finsbury Park (Lowman, 1989b).

11. A survey conducted in 1987 indicated that 47 percent of Canadians thought that prostitution should be legal (45 percent thought that it should not) and that the greatest support for legalized prostitution was in Vancouver (Fleischman, 1989: 103); 71 percent of respondents to this survey, however, thought that the meetings of prostitutes and their customers on city streets should be a criminal offence.

12. One example of such disparity relates to abortion law in Canada. Access to abortion is established by local hospital boards. Depending on the membership of the board, hospitals become either pro- or anti-abortion. The result is considerable regional and local variation in access to abortion and considerable expense and hardship for women seeking abortions in areas dominated by anti-abortion boards.

13. From a conversation with Bob Menzies.

References

Burstyn, V. (ed.) (1985) *Women against Censorship*. Toronto: Douglas and McIntyre.

Cain, M. (1985) 'Beyond informal justice', *Contemporary Crises*, 9: 335–73.

Canadian Sentencing Commission (1987) Ottawa: Government Publishers.

Christie, N. (1977) 'Conflicts as property', *British Journal of Criminology*, 17: 1–14.

Cohen, J. (1985) *Visions of Social Control*. Cambridge: Polity Press.

Cohen, S. (1987) 'Taking decentralization seriously: values, visions and policies', in J. Lowman, R.J. Menzies and T.S. Palys (eds), *Transcarceration: Essays in the Sociology of Social Control*. Aldershot: Gower. pp. 358–79.

Cohen, S. (1988) *Against Criminology*. Oxford: Transaction Books.

Dekeseredy, W.S. and Schwartz, M.D. (1991) 'Left realism and woman abuse: a critical appraisal', in R. Quinney and H. Pepinsky (eds), *Criminology as Peacemaking*. Bloomington: Indiana University Press.

Doob, A. (1990) 'Sentencing reform commissions: learning from other jurisdictions'. Paper presented at the conference on Criminal Justice: Sentencing Issues and Reforms, University of Saskatchewan, 15–16 March.

Doob, A. and Roberts, J.V. (1983) *An Analysis of the Public's View of Sentencing*. Ottawa: Department of Justice.

Fleischman, J. (1989) *Street Prostitution, Assessing the Impact of the Law: Synthesis Report*. Ottawa: Department of Justice.

Garland, D. (1987) 'Review of Richard Kinsey, John Lea and Jock Young, *Losing the Fight Against Crime*', *Contemporary Crises*, 11(2): 198–201.

Hulsman, L. (1986) 'Critical criminology and the concept of crime', *Contemporary Crises*, 10: 63–80.

Iadicola, P. (1986) 'Community crime control strategies', *Crime and Social Justice*, 25: 140–165.

Jones, T., MacLean, B. and Young, J. (1986) *The Islington Crime Survey: Crime, Victimization and Policy in Inner City London*. Aldershot: Gower.

Keat, R. and Urry, J. (1976) *Social Theory as Science*. London: Routledge & Kegan Paul.

Kinsey, R., Lea, J. and Young, J. (1986) *Losing the Fight against Crime*. Oxford: Blackwell.

Krajick, K. (1979) 'Preventing Crime', *Police Magazine*, November.

Lea, J. (1987) 'Left realism: a defence', *Contemporary Crises*, 11: 357–71.

Lea, J. and Young, J. (1984) *What is to be Done About Law and Order?* Harmondsworth: Penguin in association with the Socialist Society.

Lowman, J. (1986) 'Street prostitution in Vancouver: some notes on the genesis of a social problem', *Canadian Journal of Criminology*, 28(1): 1–16.

Lowman, J. (1989a) *Street Prostitution, Assessing the Impact of the Law: Vancouver*. Ottawa: Department of Justice.

Lowman, J. (1989b) 'Prostitution in Canada: some reflections on the logic of left regulationism'. Paper presented at the British Criminology Conference, Bristol, 17–20 July.

Lowman, J. (1990) 'The "left regulation" of prostitution: reconciling individual and collective interests'. Paper presented at the conference on Realist Criminology: Setting the Agenda for Crime Control and Policing in the 1990s, Vancouver, 24–5 May.

Matthews, R. (1986) *Policing Prostitution: A Multi-agency Approach*. Middlesex Polytechnic Centre for Criminology, Paper 1.

Matthews, R. (1987) 'Taking realist criminology seriously', *Contemporary Crises*, 11: 371–401.

Matthews, R. and Young, J. (1986) *Confronting Crime*. London: Sage.

Platt, A. (1978) 'Street crime: a view from the left', *Crime and Social Justice*, 9: 26–34.

Rafter, N.H. (1986) 'Left out by the left: crime and crime control', *Socialist Review*, 16(5): 7–23.

Scheerer, S. (1986) 'Towards abolitionism', *Contemporary Crises*, 10: 5–20.

Taylor, I. (1981) *Law and Order: Arguments for Socialism*. London: Macmillan.

Taylor, I., Walton, P. and Young, J. (1973) *The New Criminology for a Social Theory of Deviance*. London: Routledge & Kegan Paul.

Taylor, I., Walton, P. and Young, J. (1975) 'Critical criminology in Britain: review and prospects', in I. Taylor, P. Walton and J. Young (eds), *Critical Criminology*. London: Routledge & Kegan Paul.

Thompson, E.P. (1977) *Whigs and Hunters: The Origins of the Black Act*. Harmondsworth: Penguin.

Ward, R. and Ryan, T. (1989) 'Left realism against the left revisited, or some particularities of the British', in W. Rolston and M. Tomlinson (eds), *Justice and Ideology: Strategies for the 1990s*. The European Group for the Study of Deviance and Social Control Working Paper No. 9.

Young, J. (1975) 'Working class criminology', in I. Taylor, P.Walton and J. Young (eds), *Critical Criminology*. London: Routledge & Kegan Paul. pp. 63–94.

Young, J. (1979) 'Left idealism, reformism and beyond: from new criminology to Marxism', in National Deviancy Conference/Conference of Socialist Economists (eds), *Capitalism and the Rule of Law*. London: Hutchinson. pp. 11–28.

Young, J. (1986) 'The failure of criminology: the need for a radical realism', in R. Matthews and J. Young (eds), *Confronting Crime*. London: Sage. pp. 4–30.

Young, J. (1987) 'The tasks facing a realist criminology', *Contemporary Crises*, 11: 337–56.

Index